GRAND TRADITIONS

GRAND HOTEL   POINT CLEAR, ALABAMA

GRAND TRADITIONS

GRAND HOTEL ♦ POINT CLEAR, ALABAMA

Published by
PCH Hotels and Resorts, Inc.

Copyright © 2009 The Grand Hotel
PCH Hotels and Resorts, Inc.
One Grand Boulevard
Point Clear, Alabama 36564

Executive Editor: Michael Herzog, Director of Food and Beverage

Front jacket photograph and pages 21, 24, 26, 28–29, 31, 35, 46, 48, 52–53, 54, 57, 59, 67, 72, 84–85, 96, 106, 107, 108–109, 110, 112–13, 119, 122, 129, 130–31, 133, 134, 137, 142, 144–145 © by Mike Rutherford
Historical and archival (black and white and color) photography sourced by the Grand Hotel

Library of Congress Control Number: 2009902619
ISBN: 978-0-9822393-0-8

Edited, Designed, and Produced by

FRP.INC

A wholly owned subsidiary of Southwestern/Great American, Inc.
P.O. Box 305142
Nashville, Tennessee 37230
1-800-358-0560

Editorial Director: Mary Cummings
Project Editor: Jane Hinshaw
Art Direction and Book Design: Starletta Polster

Manufactured in the United States of America
First Printing 2009
10,000 copies

PREFACE

The book title tells it all: "Grand Traditions." The creation of the book comes from the inspiring history, traditions both new and old, and the people who created both. We have also included throughout the book food and beverage recipes and stories about the wonderful amenities the resort has to offer.

The narrative that is spread throughout the book includes many historical facts and how the hotel played an important role in shaping them.

Traditions are started every day with someone's first visit and are continued with returning guests celebrating a fiftieth anniversary. Some traditions like afternoon tea have existed for many years, while others like the firing of the Civil War cannon are only a year old.

The purpose of the book is to share with everyone a good taste of what the Grand Hotel is all about. Please enjoy and share with friends and family.

ACKNOWLEDGMENTS

A hotel is not a hotel without staff and therefore writing acknowledgments about individuals is a near-impossible task. Thousands of people over the 170 years of the hotel's existence have contributed to the Grand Hotel either as guests, associates, or owners. We want to thank each and every person for contributing to this incredible resort.

The idea of creating a book about the Grand Hotel has been a topic of conversation for many years, and it is important to recognize the team of individuals that helped to complete the task. Chef Mike Wallace, Debbie "the Decorator" Weeks-Badalamenti, Beth Hargett, Susan "Pack Rat" Stein, Sue Heidelberg, Edwin Torres, Ashley Haeusler, Michael Herzog, and Benjamin Hoeb. Without their tireless effort this book would not have become a reality.

Special thanks to all the photographers and contributors over the years who helped to capture the essence of the Grand Hotel. Photographers include Hagood, Tad Denson, Cotton Printing, Charlie Sefried, Renaissance Photography, Renner Photography, Daniel Vaughn Photography, Jubilee Photography, USA Archives, Museum of Mobile, Thigpen Photography, and Kaufner Photography.

Finally, thank you to the current ownership, the Retirement Systems of Alabama. Through their commitment and vision and the leadership of Dr. David Bronner, Chief Executive Officer, the Grand Hotel Marriott Resort, Golf Club, and Spa is better than ever.

Hilbert Locke, Al Agee, Jr., and Chester Hunt

THE TRADITION OF SOUTHERN HOSPITALITY

Smile and everyone smiles back, especially our friendly staff. They truly enjoy being a part of the Grand Tradition. As expressed by one long-term associate, "Our service makes guests feel right at home." Some of our associates have worked here for thirty, forty, and even fifty years, and for some working at the Grand is a family tradition, too! Dedication to customer service and exceeding guest expectations is a way of life at the Grand for our hundreds of associates.

"Our service makes guests feel right at home."

The gentlemen pictured include Al Agee, Jr., who is one of three generations and will celebrate his fiftieth year in fall 2009, Chester Hunt, who worked here for sixty-three years, and Hilbert Locke, who still greets guests on the front drive, is working on his fifty-second year. Al Agee, Jr., has said, "Work hard and learn as much as you can. Don't give up if you have a bad day, because the next day will be better!" Al's father, Al Agee, Sr., worked at the golf club for about fifty years, and Al's son, Al Agee III, is currently greeting guests at the clubhouse. Al Agee, Jr., worked as dishwasher, waiter, bartender, dining room manager, security officer, head bellman, gate attendant, and spa attendant, to name a few. One of his favorite memories is being private aide to Governor George Wallace during his stay.

Hilbert Locke began working in April 1954 on the front drive as a bellman, and he continues to greet guests to this day. Hilbert's Spirit to Serve award exemplifies exceptional customer service. He has been described by our many repeat guests as someone who gives a personal level of truly welcoming and who "puts the enthusiasm and true meaning of customer service into all his actions."

Chester Hunt, longtime waiter, bellman, and historian, began his storied career in 1941. He is recognized as one of "Alabama's Unforgettable Faces." He says, "My greatest satisfaction is meeting people from all over the world as they pass through our doors."

Other long-term associates include Ms. Inez Shepard, "Uncle Bud" Allen, Bucky Miller, Eddie Allen, Maggie Allen, Curtis Bosby, Sam Bradley, Alice Campbell, Veryl Coleman, Joyce Dailey, Annie Dennis, Morris Dennis, Dot Finkley, Lottie Forrest, Rosie Lee James, Vicky Kostelecky, Clinton Lewis, Marie Malone, Pat McCants, April "Prillie" Mullins, Thelma Scott, Sam Sealy, Vergie Smith, Lillie Thomas, Pat Thompkins, Burnell Wasp, Alice Watts, Thomas Watts, and Annie Williams.

THE GRAND HOTEL TIME LINE

1771 – Point Clear is referred to as Point Grandingo on a British map.

1847 – F. H. Chamberlain builds the second Grand Hotel. It includes a separate building with a bar called "The Texas," so-called because Texas stood apart from the nation in early days.

1770s	1830s	1840s	1850s

1830s – The cotton gin was invented. Boats were run by steam. The first Grand Hotel was built at Point Clear.

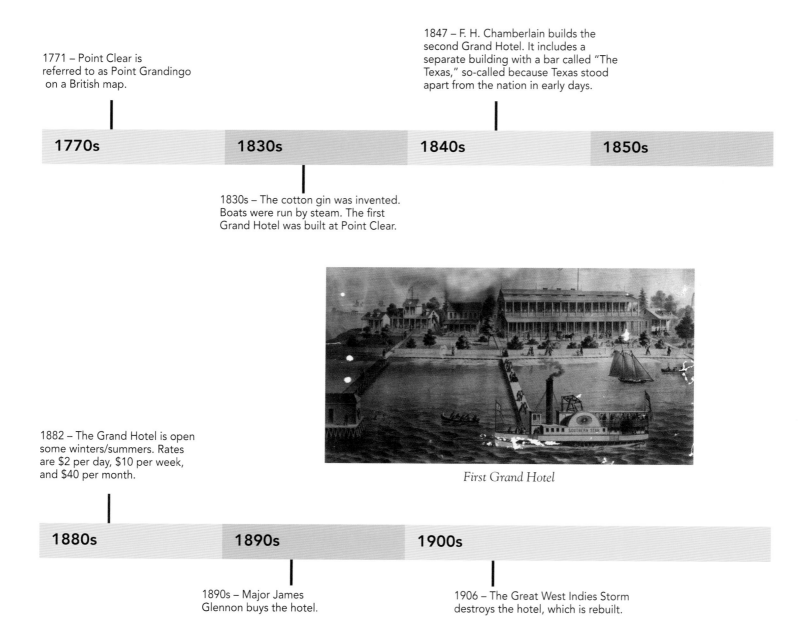

First Grand Hotel

1882 – The Grand Hotel is open some winters/summers. Rates are $2 per day, $10 per week, and $40 per month.

1880s	1890s	1900s

1890s – Major James Glennon buys the hotel.

1906 – The Great West Indies Storm destroys the hotel, which is rebuilt.

Aug. 1864 – The Battle of Mobile Bay. Admiral Farragut brought his Union fleet into Mobile Bay to defeat the Confederate fleet.

Aug. 27,1871 – The steamboat *Ocean Wave* explodes at the wharf. The "Texas" bar is used as a hospital.

1875 – Captain Henry Baldwin builds another Grand Hotel for $75,000.

1860s

1870s

1860s – After the Battle of Vicksburg, the hotel is used for a Civil War hospital.

Second Grand Hotel

1916 – Two hurricanes hit the hotel on July 5 & October 18.

1910s

1930s

1917 – The Grand Hotel has its own ice plant and electric lights.

1939 – E. A. Roberts buys the hotel with plans for a golf course.

THE GRAND HOTEL TIME LINE

1940 – The old building is demolished and a new one is built with 84 guest rooms. The new Grand Hotel features air-conditioning.

1947 – The Grand Hotel reopens and two nine-hole courses, Azalea and Dogwood, are open at the Lakewood Golf Club. There were two gondolas on the lagoon where guests could watch the beautiful black swans.

1940s

1950s

July 1944 – The hotel is used by the military as a training base for the Army Air Corps. To protect the hardwood floors, the soldiers were not allowed to wear combat boots in the building.

1959 – All-Star Golf televised golf events at the Lakewood Club. Jimmy Demeret was the commentator.

Third Grand Hotel

1990s

2000s

1997 – The Grand Hotel celebrates 150 years.

1999 – Point Clear Holdings buys the Grand Hotel with financing by the Retirement Systems of Alabama.

2003 – Major renovations are completed to include a new 20,000-square-foot European-style spa, pool, and additional guest rooms.

1967 – The Conference Center
is added at the hotel.

1981 – Marriott Corporation acquires
and adds marina building and north
bayhouse to the resort.

1960s

1980s

1980 – The Grand Hotel recovers
from Hurricane Frederic. Repairs
cost about $4 million.

1986 – The Old Gunnison House is taken
down and the Grand Ballroom is added. An
additional nine-hole golf course is added for
a total of thirty-six holes.

Current Grand Hotel

2000s

August 2005 – The hotel closes after
major damage from Hurricane Katrina.

November 2006 – The Grand Hotel
reopens with a $50 million
renovation after Hurricane Katrina.

2009 – The Grand Hotel
continues to maintain its long-
standing traditions.

LAKEWOOD GOLF CLUB

Nestled directly on the Grand Hotel's property is the Lakewood Golf Club. In 1944, Edward A. Roberts, CEO of the Waterman Steamship Company and owner of the Grand Hotel, had planned the opening of a beautiful eighteen-hole golf course to go along with the hotel renovations after World War II. Perry Maxwell of Oklahoma City had begun laying out the course, making sure to extend the golf trail through old oaks, magnolias, pines, and dogwoods. The two nine-hole courses, Azalea and Dogwood, were completed in May of 1947 and opened a month later. Early on in its history, Lakewood hosted many of golf's greatest legends, such as Sam Snead, Bobby Locke, George Bayer, Tommy Bolt, George Fazio, Billy Casper, and Patty Berg. It also hosted frequent celebrity golfers, including Bob Hope, President Gerald Ford, and beloved University of Alabama football coach Paul "Bear" Bryant.

"Lakewood consists of two eighteen-hole courses called Azalea and Dogwood."

Lakewood received a great deal of attention in 1959 when All-Star Golf was introduced. This made-for-television event featured Jimmy Demeret as commentator, with several legendary golfers participating. Most matches had winners taking home the championship prize of $2,000. Also during this time, home sites were made available and residences began emerging on the golf course. This brought along an extensive membership that is still thriving today.

Today, Lakewood consists of two eighteen-hole courses still called Azalea and Dogwood. Both golf courses collectively received millions of dollars for renovations by golf architect Bobby Vaughan, who played a pivotal role in creating the famous Robert Trent Jones Golf Trail in Alabama. The Dogwood course winds its way toward the hotel and Mobile Bay, featuring an abundance of water and narrow, tree-lined fairways. The Azalea course flows through Point Clear's woods, displaying magnificent oak trees and conveniently placed bunkers. The legendary Lakewood Clubhouse also went through an exquisite restoration in 2008 with a new golf shop and dining area.

The McLean Room

The Lakewood membership has long enjoyed the relaxing setting of the McLean Room at the Lakewood Clubhouse. Named after J. K. (Jim) McLean, the owner of the Grand Hotel from 1961–1981, this cozy, members-only lounge with a deck and card room has been an ideal place for members to enjoy each other and share stories.

LAKEWOOD SALAD DRESSING

1 small onion, chopped
1 garlic clove, chopped
2 cups mayonnaise
1 cup sandwich sauce (tested with Durkee
    Famous Sandwich and Salad Sauce)

1 tablespoon Worcestershire sauce
1 teaspoon sugar
$1/2$ teaspoon salt
$1/2$ teaspoon white pepper
Half-and-half

Combine the onion, garlic, mayonnaise, sandwich sauce, Worcestershire sauce, sugar, salt and white pepper in a blender. Process until smooth. Add enough half-and-half to make the desired consistency, processing constantly. Chill before serving. Serve over salad, lump crab meat or shrimp.

Makes 1 quart

LAKEWOOD RIBS

3 tablespoons chili powder
2 tablespoons onion powder
2 tablespoons garlic powder
1 tablespoon paprika
1 tablespoon celery salt
2 teaspoons smoked sea salt

1 teaspoon pepper
$1/4$ cup brandy
$1/4$ cup olive oil
1 tablespoon liquid smoke
5 racks pork baby back ribs
Jack Daniel's Barbecue Sauce (page 17)

Mix the chili powder, onion powder, garlic powder, paprika, celery salt, sea salt and pepper in a bowl. Add the brandy, olive oil and liquid smoke and mix well to make a rib slurry.

Rub the rib slurry on both sides of the rib racks. Wrap each rack individually in foil. Marinate in the refrigerator for 2 to 3 hours.

Place the foil-wrapped ribs in a roasting pan and roast in a preheated 275-degree oven for 3 to 4 hours or until the meat is almost falling off the bones.

Remove the ribs from the foil and coat generously with Jack Daniel's Barbecue Sauce. Grill over medium heat until caramelized on both sides.

Serves 10

JACK DANIEL'S BARBECUE SAUCE

1/2 large onion, chopped
2 tablespoons chopped garlic
Olive oil for sautéing
1/4 cup tomato paste
1/3 cup Jack Daniel's whiskey
2 cups ketchup
3/4 cup packed brown sugar
1/2 cup chili sauce
1/2 cup orange juice

1/3 cup cider vinegar
1/3 cup molasses
1/4 cup Worcestershire sauce
1 tablespoon liquid smoke
1 tablespoon Tabasco sauce, or to taste
1/2 tablespoon chili powder
1/2 tablespoon salt
1/2 teaspoon pepper

Sauté the onion and garlic in a small amount of olive oil in a saucepan for 1 to 2 minutes or until translucent. Stir in the tomato paste and cook for 1 to 2 minutes. Add the whiskey carefully and allow to ignite, if possible. Cook until heated through or until the flames subside.

Add the ketchup, brown sugar, chile sauce, orange juice, cider vinegar, molasses, Worcestershire sauce, liquid smoke, Tabasco sauce, chili powder, salt and pepper; mix well.

Bring the sauce to a boil. Reduce the heat to low and simmer for 20 minutes, stirring constantly. Process in a food processor if a smoother sauce is preferred.

Makes 5 cups

The Grand Hotel has always been at the forefront of culinary excellence. From the beginning, the hotel served breakfast, lunch, and dinner to every hotel guest, as the cost of the meal was incorporated in the rate of their hotel rooms. When the hotel added more guest sleeping rooms, the restaurant expanded to accommodate all the guests who dined.

During dinner, a coat and tie were required for gentlemen; for ladies, cocktail attire was preferred. On Saturday evenings in the mid-1900s, a tuxedo for gentlemen and formal attire for women were required. The hotel guests during these early eras treated dining as a fashion show. They were insistent upon sitting near the entrance in the middle of the room so they could observe (and be observed by) everyone wearing the latest trends in jewelry and clothing.

Throughout every decade, families have always been a focus; therefore, children were taken care of by the Junior Hostess Program. The hostesses took children to dinner separately, and they, too, were required to "dress for dinner." A fruit cup was always part of their dinner menu and still remains an option today.

As the hotel expanded rooms and the formality of the guests began to wane, the resort began focusing on having a dining room where families could feel comfortable. During this transition in the 1990s, the Grand Hotel still maintained a formal dining room, the Magnolia Room. In the 1990s, the restaurant was renamed the Bay View Restaurant, specializing in seafood dishes.

Following Hurricane Katrina, the dining room was once again renovated and the Bay View Restaurant took on the name more aptly suited for its "upscale" atmosphere, the

Grand Dining Room. The baby grand piano, which was originally in the larger casual restaurant, was placed in the Grand Dining Room, giving the restaurant a flair unlike anywhere else on the Gulf coast. The larger main dining area was then transformed into Saltwater Grill in the evening, featuring seafood specialties in an informal setting where adults and children could feel comfortable in resort attire. These two distinctly different types of restaurants enable the Grand to satisfy any culinary or service needs that a guest might have. Both the Saltwater Grill and the Grand Dining Room are surrounded by large windows that frame the view of the famous stunning sunset over Mobile Bay.

Both the Saltwater Grill and the Grand Dining Room are surrounded by large windows that frame the view of the famous stunning sunset over Mobile Bay.

The variety of dinner options at the Grand Hotel continues, as do the elaborate breakfast buffets and Sunday brunches. Family traditions have begun during these two meal periods and continue to this day. Whether a guest is having a delicious omelet made by Ms. Laura Baldwin, or a homemade Belgian waffle doused with maple syrup and whipped cream, the breakfast or brunch buffet is sure to be a memorable experience for any age.

Another dining option that remains a constant is the Pelican's Nest, serving light fare seasonally at the Grand pool. Kids and adults enjoy "lounge chair side" service as they relax around our amazing pools. Live music enhances the experience and allows your mind to drift with the tropical breezes.

Whether you're a casual diner with kids or you prefer to relax to the sound of a baby grand piano with your family, you are sure to be amazed by the multiple options the Grand Hotel provides.

GRAND TRADITIONS

MAGNOLIA BISQUE

6 ounces asparagus tips
4 ounces lobster meat, chopped
1 tablespoon minced shallot
1/2 tablespoon minced garlic
1 tablespoon olive oil
2 tablespoons white wine

6 ounces tomatoes, peeled, seeded and
   finely chopped
2 tablespoons basil chiffonade
Salt and pepper to taste
4 cups Lobster Bisque (page 50)
4 cups Asparagus Bisque (below)

Sauté the asparagus, lobster meat, shallot and garlic in the oil in a sauté pan. Add the wine and stir to loosen the brown bits from the bottom of the pan. Stir in the tomato and basil. Season with salt and pepper.

Pour 1/2 cup of the Lobster Bisque carefully into each of eight soup bowls, tilting the bowls to keep the bisque on one side. Pour 1/2 cup of the Asparagus Bisque carefully into the other side of the bowl as you place it level, trying not to mix the portions. Spoon the asparagus and lobster mixture into the center of each bowl.

Serves 8

ASPARAGUS BISQUE

2 pounds asparagus, trimmed and chopped
2 ounces shallots, chopped
1 tablespoon chopped garlic
Olive oil for sautéing
1/4 cup white wine

1 1/2 cups chicken stock
Cornstarch
Water
1 1/2 cups heavy cream
Salt and pepper to taste

Sweat the asparagus, shallots and garlic in a small amount of olive oil in a saucepan over low heat until tender. Add the wine, stirring to loosen the brown bits from the bottom of the saucepan.

Add the stock and bring to a boil. Make a slurry of three parts cornstarch and two parts water in a small bowl. Add enough of the slurry to the bisque to thicken, cooking and stirring until smooth.

Stir in the cream and simmer for 8 to 10 minutes. Season with salt and pepper. Process the bisque in a food processor or blender and strain back into the saucepan, discarding the solids. Heat to serving temperature.

Serves 10

DATE	NAME	ADDRESS
Feb 28	Mr & Mrs. N. E. Daniel	Houston, Texas
Feb 24	Lt & Mrs. Will Kill Tankersley	Montgomery, Alabama
March 6	Mr. & Mrs. Ray R. Rafferty	New Orleans, La.
March 7	Mr. & Mrs. Howard H. Amplott Jr.	Louisville, Miss.
March 8	Mr. & Mrs. C. D. Dinsbury	Laguna Beach, Cal.
29 March 54	Lt Col & Mrs. R. O. English, Jr.	Fort Benning, Ga.
April 12, 1954	Mr. & Mrs. Robert K. Weintraub	Philadelphia, Pa.
April 18, 1954	Mr. & Mrs. C. L. Paine	New York N. Y.
April 24, '54	Mr. & Mrs. E. T. Millsap Jr.	Montgomery, A.
April 24, '54	Dr. & Mrs. Jack King	Jackson, Miss.
April 25-54	Mr & Mrs. James L. Leslie	New Orleans
Apr 25, 54	Mr & Mrs Maurice M. Le Breton	New Orleans, La.
Apr 25, 54	Mr. & Mrs. Robt. W. Leeds, Jr.	Halden Hall,
Apr 30-54	Mr & Mrs. Holmes E. Penn	345 S. Drive, Los Angeles

Wedding Date

Feb 26, 1954

23 Feb 1954

march 6th

March 17th

march 6th

20 March 1954

4 - 10 - 54

4 - 10 - 54.

4 - 23 - 54

First Anniversary (week early)

April 2 &

April 24

ntic City N. April 25

April 24

HONEYMOON CELEBRATIONS AT THE GRAND HOTEL

Special occasions have been celebrated for many decades at the elegant Grand Hotel. Honeymoons are the most popular occasion, as they spark numerous traditions. The Grand Hotel displays a honeymoon book for guests to write their names and their wedding date, a tradition begun in 1951.

Major General Will Hill Tankersley met his future wife, Theda Clark Ball, in the spring of 1953. When he asked for her father's permission to marry Theda, her father refused twice but on the third attempt offered his blessing. The Tankersleys' first visit to the Grand Hotel was in February 1954, and they still return to celebrate their special day.

MILK CHOCOLATE MOUSSE NAPOLEON

Milk Chocolate Mousse
1/2 ounce unflavored gelatin
6 egg whites
1/2 cup sugar
9 egg yolks
2 cups heavy whipping cream
1 tablespoon butter
1 pound milk chocolate

Chocolate Squares
13 ounces semisweet chocolate
13 ounces milk chocolate

Assembly
Whipped cream, strawberries and
chocolate curls, for garnish

For the mousse, combine the gelatin with a small amount of cool water in a saucepan and let stand until softened. Heat over low heat until the gelatin dissolves completely, stirring constantly. Combine the egg whites with the sugar in a bowl and beat until soft peaks form. Beat the egg yolks in a bowl until light and pale yellow. Beat the whipping cream in a bowl until medium peaks form. Combine the butter and milk chocolate in a heavy saucepan. Cook over low heat until melted, stirring to blend well. Cool slightly. Add the eggs gradually, whisking constantly until smooth. Add the gelatin to the chocolate mixture and mix well. Fold the chocolate mixture gently into the beaten egg whites. Fold in the whipped cream. Spoon the mousse into a dish and chill for 1 to 2 hours.

For the squares, melt the semisweet chocolate with the milk chocolate in a saucepan over very low heat, stirring to blend well. Pour onto a baking sheet lined with baking parchment. Let stand until nearly firm. Cut into 2 1/2-inch squares with a paring knife. Let stand until firm.

To assemble, spoon the chilled mousse into a pastry bag and pipe small dollops of the mousse onto two-thirds of the chocolate squares. Stack two squares together to form each napoleon and top with the remaining squares. Garnish with whipped cream, strawberries and a chocolate curl. Store in the refrigerator.

Serves 10

Grand Hotel Dessert Trio

CHOCOLATE FLOURLESS CAKE

1 cup (2 sticks) butter
1/2 cup milk
1/2 cup sugar
8 ounces chocolate, chopped
4 eggs, beaten

Melt the butter in a saucepan. Add the milk and sugar and mix well. Heat to a simmer. Add the chocolate and stir until melted and blended. Remove from the heat and whisk in the eggs gradually. Cool to room temperature. Spoon into greased nonstick muffin cups.

Bake in a preheated 350-degree oven for 12 to 15 minutes or until the cakes test done. Cool in the muffin cups for 5 minutes. Loosen with a knife and remove. Frost or garnish as desired and serve warm or cooled.

Serves 10

WHITE AND DARK CHOCOLATE SHOOTERS

White Chocolate Shooter
1 cup (or more) heavy cream
$1/4$ cup sugar
1 to 2 ounces white chocolate liqueur
(tested with Godiva)
$1/4$ vanilla bean, or 1 teaspoon
vanilla extract
$1/2$ cup white chocolate

Dark Chocolate Shooter
1 cup (or more) heavy cream
$1/4$ cup sugar
1 to 2 ounces dark chocolate liqueur
(tested with Godiva), or crème de cacao
$1/2$ cup dark chocolate

For the white chocolate shooter, combine the cream, sugar, liqueur and vanilla bean in a saucepan and bring to a boil. Remove from the heat and scrape the seeds from the vanilla pod into the mixture; discard the pod. Stir in the white chocolate until melted and well blended. Chill in the refrigerator. Serve in cordial or shot glasses, adding additional cream if needed for the desired consistency. Garnish as desired.

For the dark chocolate shooter, combine the cream, sugar and liqueur in a saucepan and bring to a boil. Remove from the heat and stir in the chocolate until melted and well blended. Chill in the refrigerator. Serve in cordial or shot glasses, adding additional cream if needed for the desired consistency. Garnish as desired.

Serves 10

THE SECRET GARDEN

A tradition that began in 2006, the Secret Garden was created with one thing in mind . . . romance. Overlooking the Chef's Garden and the beautiful Mobile Bay sunset, the Secret Garden has been a perfect "secret" hideaway for many special occasions. Guests have celebrated birthdays, anniversaries, Valentine's Day, and proposals in the Secret Garden. Each memory that has been created is documented in the Secret Garden journal for couples to read as they dine. Fresh herbs and vegetables from the garden are used in the preparation of the Secret Garden menus. We have included a sample of one of our menus, which would be perfect for a romantic Valentine's Day dinner or a delicious meal with the special person in your life.

FROM THE SECRET GARDEN JOURNAL

13 October 2007 ~ Saturday

We hope those who dine in the Secret Garden after us have an amazing of a night as we have had!

Our special night started one year ago with a kiss between friends. Over the past year we have fallen in love and chose to celebrate our anniversary at The Grand. While I enjoyed a relaxing day at the pool, David was sneeky and made plans for the evening.

For those who came before, this may have been an amazing dinner, but for us its the beginning of the rest of our lives together. During the last course of our fabulous meal, David dropped to one knee and asked me to be his wife. For hidden within the dessert was the most beautiful ring ever! I said yes!

Thanks to everyone at The Grand who made this the most memorable night of our lives!

Enjoyed the evening,

Melanie + David

Menu

Asian Tuna Amusé
Moët & Chandon White Star Champagne

Magnolia Bisque

Baby Iceberg Salad

Fresh Lump Gulf Crab Cake

Rose Petal & Vanilla Sorbet
Intermezzo

Grilled Kobe Beef Filet
accompanied by Cabernet Potatoes,
Glazed Baby Carrots
and a Port Wine Demi-Glace

Grand Hotel Dessert Trio

Chocolate Truffle Mignardise

BABY ICEBERG SALAD

15 figs
3 tablespoons white balsamic vinegar
2 tablespoons light corn syrup
1 tablespoon blend of 4 parts canola oil
to 1 part extra-virgin olive oil

Salt and pepper to taste
5 heads baby iceberg lettuce
Goat Cheese Dressing (below)
Fried Shallot Garnish (page 33)

Combine the figs with the balsamic vinegar, corn syrup, oil blend, salt and pepper in a bowl and mix well. Place in a roasting pan. Roast in a preheated 350-degree oven for 5 to 6 minutes or until lightly glazed and brown. Cut the figs into quarters.

Cut off the brown ends of the lettuce stems, leaving the stems intact. Cut the lettuces into halves through the stem ends. Rinse and drain the lettuce well. Cut off a small slice on the rounded sides so the lettuce halves will stand firmly on the plates. Place on serving plates and arrange the fig quarters around the lettuce. Drizzle with Goat Cheese Dressing. Top with Fried Shallot Garnish.

Serves 10

GOAT CHEESE DRESSING

1 teaspoon chopped parsley
1 teaspoon chopped shallot
1/4 teaspoon dried dill weed
1/4 teaspoon onion powder
1/4 teaspoon garlic powder
1/4 teaspoon onion salt

1/4 teaspoon garlic salt
1 cup mayonnaise
1 cup buttermilk
3 ounces goat cheese
1/8 teaspoon white pepper

Combine the parsley, shallot, dill weed, onion powder, garlic powder, onion salt and garlic salt in a blender. Add the mayonnaise, buttermilk, goat cheese and white pepper. Process until smooth. Serve over Baby Iceberg Salad (above).

Serves 10

FRIED SHALLOT GARNISH

5 shallots
$1/2$ cup all-purpose flour
$1/4$ teaspoon Cajun seasoning
$1/4$ teaspoon salt
$1/8$ teaspoon pepper
Vegetable oil for frying

Slice the shallots very thinly. Mix the flour, Cajun seasoning, salt and pepper in a bowl. Add the shallots and toss to coat well; shake off any excess flour mixture. Fry in a skillet in vegetable oil preheated to 350 degrees until golden brown; drain. Serve over Baby Iceberg Salad (page 32).

Serves 10

FOSSIL POTATO CHIPS

10 large potatoes
Tarragon leaves
Sliced chives

Cut the potatoes into $2^{1}/2$-inch cubes. Slice the cubes thinly on a vegetable slicer or mandoline. Arrange half the potato slices on a nonstick baking pan. Arrange tarragon leaves and chives on each piece. Top with the remaining potato slices and a second baking pan. Bake in a preheated 250-degree oven for 15 to 20 minutes or until brown. Use as a garnish for the Kobe Beef Filet (page 34).

Serves 10

KOBE BEEF FILET

1/4 cup olive oil
1 tablespoon minced garlic
1 tablespoon minced rosemary
10 (6-ounce) Kobe beef filets or other beef filets
White asparagus and chive stems, for garnish

Combine the olive oil, garlic and rosemary in a sealable plastic bag. Add the beef and mix well. Marinate in the refrigerator for 3 hours or longer. Sear the beef on the grill or in a sauté pan. Place in a roasting pan and roast in a preheated 375-degree oven to the desired internal temperature. Garnish with spears of white asparagus tied into a bundle with chive stems. Serve with Cabernet Potatoes (below), Baby Carrots with Vanilla Bean Gastrique (page 36) and Fossil Potato Chips (page 33) on a plate napped with Port Wine Sauce (page 36).

Serves 10

CABERNET POTATOES

1 1/2 pounds blue potatoes	1/4 cup (1/2 stick) butter
1/3 cup cabernet	Salt and pepper to taste
1/4 cup heavy cream	

Peel the potatoes and cut into halves. Cook in enough water to cover in a saucepan until tender. Simmer the wine in a saucepan over low to medium heat until reduced by one-half. Combine the cream and butter in a 2-quart saucepan and bring to a simmer. Drain the potatoes and add the wine reduction and the cream mixture. Mash the potatoes until smooth. Season with salt and pepper.

Serves 10

BABY CARROTS WITH VANILLA BEAN GASTRIQUE

$^1/_2$ cup water
$^1/_2$ cup sugar
$^1/_2$ vanilla bean, split
40 baby carrots, cut into
halves lengthwise

2 tablespoons butter
Salt and pepper to taste

Combine $^1/_2$ cup water with the sugar in a saucepan. Add the vanilla bean and simmer for 8 to 10 minutes for the vanilla bean gastrique. Let stand until cool. Scrape the seeds from the vanilla pod into the syrup with a spoon; discard the pod. Blanch the carrots in enough water to cover in a saucepan; drain. Sauté the carrots in a small amount of butter in a saucepan. Add the vanilla bean gastrique and sauté until glazed. Season with salt and pepper.

Serves 10

PORT WINE SAUCE

1 sprig of parsley
1 sprig of thyme
1 sprig of rosemary
1 bay leaf
$^1/_2$ cup port
2 tablespoons chopped shallots

1 tablespoon minced garlic
3 cups Demi-Glace (page 37)
Cornstarch
Water
2 tablespoons butter
$^1/_4$ cup port

Tie the parsley, thyme, rosemary and bay leaf together with kitchen twine to make a bouquet garni. Combine with $^1/_2$ cup wine, the shallots and garlic in a small saucepan. Cook over low heat until the wine is reduced by three-fourths. Add the Demi-Glace and cook until reduced by one-fourth. Remove the bouquet garni. Make a slurry of three parts cornstarch and two parts water in a small bowl. Add enough to the sauce to thicken to the desired consistency, stirring constantly. Stir in the butter and $^1/_4$ cup wine.

Makes 2$^1/_2$ cups

DEMI-GLACE

3 pounds veal bones	1 sprig of parsley
3 ribs celery, coarsely chopped	1 sprig of thyme
2 carrots, coarsely chopped	1 sprig of rosemary
1 small onion, coarsely chopped	1 bay leaf
$1/3$ cup tomato paste	6 cups water
$1/3$ cup red wine	1 teaspoon black peppercorns

Place the veal bones in a roasting pan. Roast, uncovered, in a preheated 450-degree oven for 45 minutes or until light brown. Add the celery, carrots and onion and mix well. Roast until the vegetables are golden brown. Stir in the tomato paste. Roast until the vegetables are caramelized and turning very dark around the edges.

Add the wine and stir to loosen the brown bits from the bottom of the roasting pan. Pour the mixture into a stockpot. Tie the parsley, thyme, rosemary and bay leaf together with kitchen twine to make a bouquet garni. Add to the stockpot with the water and peppercorns. Simmer over very low heat for 8 hours or longer.

Strain into a second stockpot and simmer until reduced by one-half; skim the surface every hour. Strain into a storage container to use in soups, sauces or ragoût.

Serves 10

THE EASTERN SHORE AND FAIRHOPE

One of the most attractive features of the Grand Hotel is the surrounding Eastern Shore of the Mobile Bay. A series of towns make up the Eastern Shore, including Spanish Fort, Daphne, Montrose, Fairhope, and Point Clear.

Fairhope is one of two single tax colonies; the other is in Arden, Delaware. In 1894, a group from Des Moines, Iowa, headed by Ernest B. Gaston, wanted to establish a colony based on the single tax theories of Henry George. In 1879, his ideologies were published in his book, *Progress and Poverty*. About 4,500 acres of land in and around Fairhope is owned by the Fairhope Single Tax Corporation. This includes the downtown area and a little less than half of the remainder of the city.

When entering the town of Fairhope, the first thing one might notice is the bright array of fragrant flowers and the large live oaks that adorn the parks and roadways. The Eastern Shore and Fairhope have long been known as a haven for artists and writers, attracting energetic, eclectic, and engaging personalities from around the South and beyond. The diverse mix of chic boutiques and vibrant restaurants ensures that there's no end to what you will discover throughout the region.

There is Mardi Gras, of course, which was first celebrated in the New World in the nearby city of Mobile. Each of the surrounding towns celebrates with parades and balls in the pre-Lenten festival.

Fairhope has a world-renowned Arts and Crafts Festival, celebrated every March. Polo at the Point occurs in the late spring and early fall.

Hiking trails beginning at the Grand Hotel extend from Point Clear all the way to the U.S.S. *Alabama*, thirty-two miles away.

There is so much to see and do on the Eastern Shore: water, beaches, walking trails, shopping, history, arts, sports, a unique lifestyle, and an environment unlike any other.

Civil War Cannon at the Grand

On display at the Grand Hotel is a reproduction of a Confederate bronze 6-pounder smoothbore cannon originally made in 1862 by the Tredegar Iron Works, Richmond, Virginia. Under the direction of Joseph Reid Anderson, owner and operator of the Tredegar Iron Works at the time the South seceded from the Union, the 6-pounder cannon was copied from a Model 1841 Union bronze 6-pounder. The cannon on display fired a six-pound projectile using $1^{1}/4$ pounds of black powder with a maximum range of 1,523 yards at 5 degrees elevation. The 6-pounder gun was able to fire solid shot, spherical case shot, and canister.

THE CANNON

In spring 2008, a new tradition started at the Grand Hotel. Each afternoon a cannon is fired to salute today's military and those who have passed through the historic hotel over the years. The daily ceremony starts with a procession of a military band, including drums and horns, marching around the property. It ends at Cannon Park, where a historian tells the story of military history at the Grand Hotel and then fires the cannon.

When the War Between the States broke out in 1861, the South found out quickly that it was at a disadvantage to the Union since most industrial facilities needed for goods, from shipbuilding to everyday items such as salt, meat, clothing, and, most importantly, weapons, were located in the North.

By 1863, large blockade-runners could operate in and out of only four ports, one of them being Mobile, Alabama.

In an attempt to counteract the Union navy, the Confederates introduced the underwater torpedo. Underwater torpedoes were the new invisible weapon and were widely used at the entrance to Mobile Bay to aid the blockade-runners in their delivery of goods to the port of Mobile.

"Underwater torpedoes were the new invisible weapon and were widely used at the entrance to Mobile Bay to aid the blockade-runners in their delivery of goods to the port of Mobile."

On August 5, 1864, Admiral Farragut led a rather large Union naval fleet into Mobile Bay to block the delivery of goods. They were met at the pass between Fort Morgan on the eastern side of the bay and Fort Gaines on the western side with a barrage of torpedoes. One torpedo hit the "unsinkable" ironclad, the *Tecumseh*, sinking it in two minutes.

This infuriated Admiral Farragut, but he was determined to stop the blockade-runners. This is when he made the famous statement, "Damn the torpedoes, full speed ahead!" Over the next three weeks Farragut's vessels and the Union army finally forced the defenders of Fort Morgan to surrender. The port of Mobile was then closed to blockade-runners, but the city of Mobile remained in Confederate hands until 1865.

During this time, the Grand Hotel was turned into a base hospital and was guarded by a garrison of the 21st Alabama Infantry. Most of those sent to the Grand Hotel for recovery were soldiers from Mississippi who were injured during the Battle of Vicksburg in 1863. This battle took place in Vicksburg, Mississippi, some 250 miles away from the Grand Hotel.

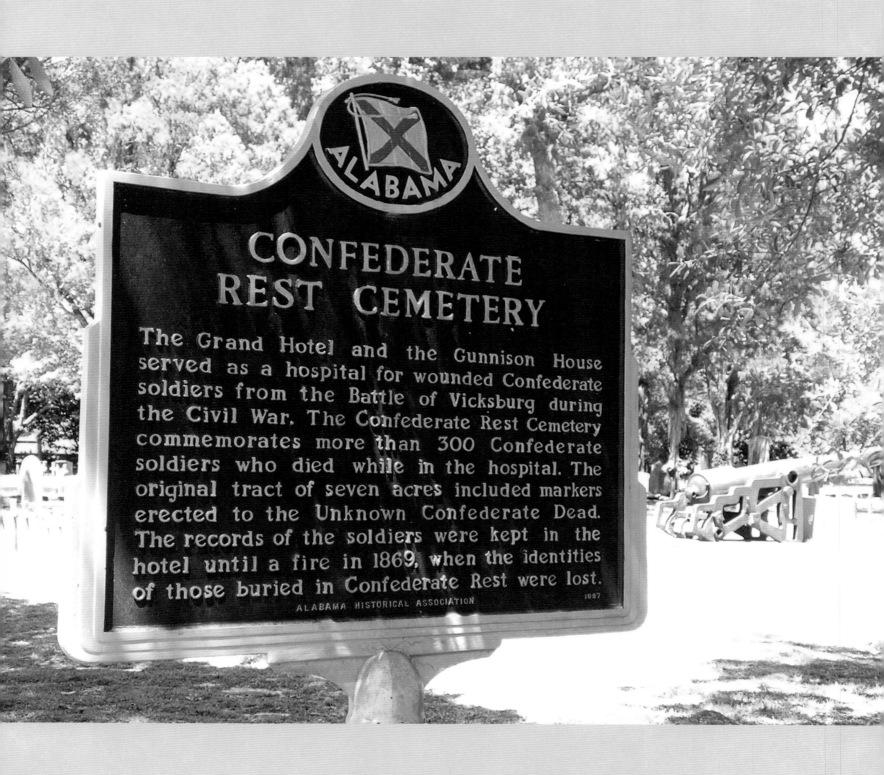

CONFEDERATE REST CEMETERY

The Grand Hotel and the Gunnison House served as a hospital for wounded Confederate soldiers from the Battle of Vicksburg during the Civil War. The Confederate Rest Cemetery commemorates more than 300 Confederate soldiers who died while in the hospital. The original tract of seven acres included markers erected to the Unknown Confederate Dead. The records of the soldiers were kept in the hotel until a fire in 1869, when the identities of those buried in Confederate Rest were lost.

ALABAMA HISTORICAL ASSOCIATION   1997

More than three hundred Confederate soldiers died while in the hospital at the Grand Hotel. These soldiers are buried in Confederate Rest, a cemetery adjacent to the hotel grounds near the Lakewood Golf Club. The soldiers were buried shoulder to shoulder in mass graves. The records of the soldiers were kept in the hotel until a fire in 1869, when the identities of those buried in Confederate Rest were lost. A monument to the unknown soldiers has been placed at the cemetery. A 7-inch naval gun used at Fort Morgan has been mounted at Confederate Rest, along with a commemorative plaque. A fence topped with cannonballs surrounds the marker.

Admiral Farragut indeed fired weapons on the Grand Hotel grounds. A hole was found in the wall of the Gunnison House, which is the site of the Grand's Conference Center today. While the Gunnison House was being torn down years ago, writing near that hole stated, "Compliments of Admiral Farragut."

CONFEDERATE REST, POINT CLEAR, ALA.

LUMP CRAB SCRAMBLE

2 tablespoons finely chopped tomato
1½ ounces lump crab meat
1 tablespoon finely chopped scallions
Butter for sautéing

Salt and pepper to taste
3 eggs, beaten
2 tablespoons shredded asiago cheese
Crab meat and a micro greens, for garnish

Sauté the tomato, 1½ ounces crab meat and scallions in a small amount of butter in a sauté pan. Season with salt and pepper. Add the eggs and cook until the eggs are soft-set, stirring frequently. Stir in half the cheese. Sprinkle with the remaining cheese and remove to a serving plate. Garnish with additional crab meat and micro greens.

Serves 1

THE SUNDAY BRUNCH

A tradition that locals have flocked to for decades, the Grand Hotel's Jazz Brunch has been hailed as the "Best Brunch" as long as the historic building has stood. A great place to begin the brunch experience is in the historic lobby with a glass of Bucky Miller's famous Brunch Punch. Once you enter the dining room, the Champagne generously flows as the band marches for all the guests. Chefs carve spectacular roasts and guests dine on varieties of salads, vegetables, and freshly made pastries. Miss Laura will make you one of her famous omelets, called the Lump Crab Scramble, which is listed as one of the "101 Dishes You Must Eat Before You Die." Elegance, aromas, and excitement fill the room as feet tap to the rhythm of "When the Saints Go Marching In." Complete your experience with one of the most requested desserts, the Grand Hotel Bread Pudding with Whiskey Sauce.

"The Grand Hotel's Jazz Brunch has been hailed as the 'Best Brunch' as long as the historic building has stood."

BUCKY'S GRAND HOTEL BRUNCH PUNCH

Orange juice
Pineapple juice
Apple juice
Ginger ale
Cherry juice or grenadine
Champagne

Combine equal parts of orange juice, pineapple juice and apple juice in a punch bowl. Add half as much ginger ale and mix gently. Stir in enough cherry juice or grenadine to give the desired color. Add the desired amount of Champagne and mix gently. Add ice to the punch bowl and serve.

Makes a variable amount

BREAD PUDDING

2 cups packed brown sugar
5 eggs
2 teaspoons cinnamon
1/8 teaspoon nutmeg
1/8 teaspoon ground cloves
1/4 cup bourbon

1 tablespoon vanilla extract
3 cups half-and-half
4 cups croissant cubes or dry white bread cubes
1/2 cup raisins

Combine the brown sugar, eggs, cinnamon, nutmeg and cloves in a bowl and mix well. Add the bourbon and vanilla and stir to dissolve the brown sugar completely. Stir in the half-and-half. Mix in the bread and raisins gently.

Spoon into a buttered baking dish and place in a larger pan filled halfway with hot water. Bake in a preheated 375-degree oven for 1 1/2 to 2 hours or until golden brown. Serve with Whiskey Sauce.

Serves 10

WHISKEY SAUCE

2 egg yolks
1/4 cup whiskey
1/2 cup corn syrup
1/2 cup packed brown sugar

1/4 cup granulated sugar
1/2 cup (1 stick) butter
1/2 cup water

Beat the egg yolks with the whiskey in a bowl until smooth. Combine the corn syrup, brown sugar, granulated sugar, butter and water in a saucepan and bring to a boil, stirring to mix well. Whisk 1 cup of the hot mixture gradually into the egg yolks; whisk the egg yolks gradually into the hot mixture. Bring to a gentle boil and cook until thickened and smooth, whisking constantly.

Makes 3 cups

LOBSTER BISQUE

2 pounds lobster head portions with shells
Olive oil for sautéing
2 ounces shallots, chopped
1/2 cup chopped mushrooms
1/2 cup chopped leeks
1 tablespoon chopped garlic
1/4 cup tomato paste
1/4 cup brandy
1/4 cup white wine
4 cups (1 quart) cream

2 sprigs of parsley
1 sprig of thyme
1 sprig of tarragon
1 bay leaf
1 tablespoon Cajun seasoning
1/4 teaspoon peppercorns
Salt and black pepper to taste
Pinch of cayenne pepper
Cornstarch
Water

Crush the lobster portions and sauté in a small amount of olive oil in a saucepan. Add the shallots, mushrooms, leeks and garlic and sauté for 2 minutes. Stir in the tomato paste and cook on medium-low heat for 2 minutes.

Add the brandy and wine and stir to loosen the brown bits from the bottom of the saucepan. Stir in the cream, parsley, thyme, tarragon, bay leaf, Cajun seasoning, peppercorns, salt, black pepper and cayenne pepper. Simmer for 20 minutes. Adjust the seasoning to taste and strain into a saucepan, discarding the solids.

Make a slurry of three parts cornstarch and two parts water in a small bowl. Add enough of the cornstarch slurry to the bisque just before serving to thicken it enough to coat the back of a spoon, cooking and stirring until smooth.

Serves 10

UNCLE BUD'S SEAFOOD GUMBO

1/2 cup chopped onion	1 1/2 cups chicken stock
1/2 cup chopped celery	1/2 (16-ounce) can
1/2 cup chopped green	diced tomatoes
bell pepper	1/2 (8-ounce) can
2 tablespoons	tomato sauce
bacon drippings	3 to 4 ounces brown roux
1 bay leaf	8 ounces bay shrimp
1/2 teaspoon	4 ounces shucked
oregano leaves	oysters with liquor
1/2 teaspoon	8 ounces lump crab meat
thyme leaves	8 ounces bay scallops
3 tablespoons filé powder	3/4 cup sliced okra
Pinch of cayenne pepper	Salt and pepper to taste

Sauté the onion, celery and bell pepper in the bacon drippings in a stockpot until the onion is translucent. Add the bay leaf, oregano, thyme, filé powder and cayenne pepper; mix well. Stir in the stock, undrained tomatoes and tomato sauce. Bring to a boil. Stir in the brown roux and cook until thickened, stirring constantly. Add the shrimp, oysters, crab meat, scallops and okra. Simmer until the seafood is cooked through. Season with salt and pepper. Discard the bay leaf before serving.

Serves 10

THE GRAND HOTEL GUMBO

Since the oldest mention of it by French explorer C. C. Robin, gumbo has been a food staple that is steeped in tradition around the Deep South. This tradition has been carried out by the Grand Hotel for as far back as records go. Uncle Bud, George Delbert Allen, worked for about forty-five years in the kitchen; the recipe that we recognize as his is still used today in our kitchens. The Grand Hotel Gumbo has always been a favorite among guests, and it is known that Alabama Governor George Wallace had it sent in bulk up to Montgomery.

THE CHEF'S GARDEN

Our goal has always been to have the freshest possible ingredients that we can obtain. This helped spark the creation for our own "Chef's Garden." Our plants, cultured in a greenhouse on our property, then conclude their growing process in our Chef's Garden. Throughout the year, we rotate seasonal herbs, vegetables, and fruits. This has allowed us to garnish our dishes with the most crisp, fresh micro greens. We have designed our "Hand-Crafted Cocktails" to include our garden items. This theme carries into our four-diamond-rated Grand Dining Room, where, adorning each table, we have a cachepot of herbs and vegetables. The fresh aromas of rosemary, parsley, and even peppers have added a unique touch to our ambience. You can be assured no pesticides or harmful steroids have been used in the growing process. It's our pleasure to schedule a comprehensive tour with our Horticulture Department to learn from our experts their vision, cultivation, and preservation of our Chef's Garden.

LAMB RACK

10 racks New Zealand spring lamb
3 tablespoons blackening spice
1 tablespoon minced rosemary
1 tablespoon minced garlic
1/4 cup olive oil

Swiss Chard (below)
Hoe Cakes (page 58)
Blackberry Syrup (page 56)
Zinfandel Sauce (page 56)
Rosemary sprigs, for garnish

Ask the butcher to French the ends of the lamb rib bones. Mix the blackening spice, rosemary, garlic and olive oil in a large sealable plastic bag. Add the lamb racks, turning to coat well. Marinate in the refrigerator for 2 hours.

Place the lamb on a grill heated to medium-hot. Grill for 3 to 4 minutes on each side. Remove to a roasting pan using tongs. Roast in a preheated 350-degree oven to the desired internal temperature or desired degree of doneness.

Spoon the Swiss Chard onto serving plates and top with the lamb racks and Hoe Cakes. Nap the plates with the Blackberry Syrup and serve with the Zinfandel Sauce. Garnish with sprigs of rosemary.

Serves 10

SWISS CHARD

8 cups julienned Swiss chard
2 tablespoons minced shallots
2 teaspoons minced garlic
Olive oil for sautéing

Salt and pepper to taste
2 tablespoons brandy
2 tablespoons wine

Sauté the Swiss chard, shallots and garlic in a small amount of olive oil in a sauté pan until tender. Season with salt and pepper. Mix the brandy and wine in a cup. Add to the sauté pan, stirring to loosen the brown bits from the pan. Cook until heated through.

Serves 10

ZINFANDEL SAUCE

1 sprig of parsley
1 sprig of rosemary
1 sprig of thyme
1 bay leaf
3 tablespoons chopped shallots
1 tablespoon minced garlic

1 1/4 cups zinfandel
1/2 teaspoon black peppercorns
3 cups Demi-Glace (page 37)
Cornstarch (optional)
Water (optional)
2 tablespoons butter

Tie the parsley, rosemary, thyme and bay leaf together with kitchen twine to make a bouquet garni.

Sauté the shallots and garlic in a saucepan until tender. Add the wine and stir to loosen the brown bits from the saucepan. Add the bouquet garni and peppercorns and cook until reduced by three-fourths. Stir in the Demi-Glace and cook until reduced by one-fourth.

Thicken the sauce if desired by adding a slurry of three parts cornstarch and two parts water. Cook until thickened, stirring constantly. Strain through a fine strainer into a bowl. Whisk in the butter.

Serves 10

BLACKBERRY SYRUP

1/2 cup blackberries
1/4 cup sugar
1/4 cup zinfandel

Cornstarch
Water

Combine the blackberries, sugar and wine in a saucepan. Bring to a boil and cook until reduced by one-fourth. Add a slurry of three parts cornstarch and two parts water and cook until thickened, stirring constantly. Purée in a blender or food processor and strain into a bowl, discarding the solids.

Serves 10

BABY GREENS AND GOAT CHEESE SALAD WITH STRAWBERRY-POPPY SEED VINAIGRETTE

Strawberry-Poppy Seed Vinaigrette
1/2 cup strawberries
1/2 cup sugar
1/4 cup balsamic vinegar
1/4 cup red wine vinegar
1 tablespoon lemon juice
1 tablespoon minced red onion
1/2 cup canola oil
1 tablespoon poppy seeds
Salt and pepper to taste

Baby Greens and Goat Cheese Salad
10 cups baby salad greens
10 very thin lengthwise strips of cucumber
10 round (1-ounce) slices goat cheese
1 cup strawberries, thinly sliced
Toasted pecans, for garnish

For the vinaigrette, combine the strawberries, sugar, balsamic vinegar, red wine vinegar, lemon juice and onion in a blender and process until smooth. Add the canola oil gradually, pulsing until emulsified. Combine with the poppy seeds in a bowl and mix well. Season with salt and pepper and let stand for 1 hour.

For the salad, combine the salad greens with the vinaigrette in a bowl and toss to coat evenly. Shape the cucumber slices into rings and fill with the salad. Place on serving plates and add one goat cheese slice to each plate; arrange the strawberries around the salad and garnish with toasted pecans.

Serves 10

HOE CAKES

2 cups cornmeal
1 cup all-purpose flour
2 teaspoons baking powder
3 eggs
2^1/$_2$ cups buttermilk
^{1}/$_3$ cup honey
2 tablespoons bacon drippings

^{1}/$_2$ cup corn kernels
^{1}/$_4$ cup chopped green bell pepper
^{1}/$_4$ cup chopped red bell pepper
2 to 3 tablespoons chopped onion,
    or to taste
1 teaspoon minced garlic
Additional bacon drippings

Mix the cornmeal, flour and baking powder in a bowl. Combine the eggs and buttermilk in a bowl and mix well. Add the cornmeal mixture and mix until smooth. Stir in the honey.

Heat 2 tablespoons bacon drippings in a sauté pan. Add the corn, bell peppers, onion and garlic. Sauté for 2 to 3 minutes or until the vegetables are tender. Add the sautéed vegetables to the batter and mix well.

Grease a griddle with additional bacon drippings and heat to 375 degrees. Spoon the batter onto the griddle and cook until golden brown on both sides.

Serves 10

THE GRAND MOJITO

"Hand-crafted, well-balanced cocktails made from absolutely fresh ingredients."

^{1}/$_2$ lime
3 mint leaves
2 tablespoons Simple Syrup (see page 67)
1^1/$_2$ ounces rum (tested with Bacardi)
Ice
Lime wedge and mint leaf, for garnish

Cut the lime half into three wedges. Combine the lime wedges with three mint leaves in a cocktail shaker. Muddle lightly to blend the flavors. Add the Simple Syrup and rum. Fill the shaker with ice. Seal the shaker and shake hard for 12 seconds. Pour into a highball glass and garnish with an additional lime wedge and mint leaf.

For a hand-crafted strawberry mojito (at right), muddle 3 strawberries with the lime and mint.

Serves 1

THE LIVE OAKS

The live oaks on our property are cared for by our team of tree preservation arborists to help ensure the health and beauty of some of the oldest and most valuable assets at the Grand Hotel. Young live oaks are being planted to keep the look of the beautiful trees for future generations. The grass along the bay-side boardwalk, seashore paspalum, is a "go-green" environmentally friendly grass. It can be watered with briny ocean water, which kills the weeds but doesn't harm the grass, thereby reducing the need for chemicals. As a "go-green" effort, the lagoon is stocked with koi and carp to help control the delicate balance of plant life versus water quality, again without having to rely on chemicals. Many berry-laden shrubs are found throughout the property. These shrubs provide a food source for many birds that migrate to or live at the Grand Hotel.

PAINTING 1941 - BATTLE OF MOBILE BAY

The mural depicts the start of the 1864 battle between Union and Confederate forces at the entrance of Mobile Bay.

The original painting was commissioned by the hotel's owner, E. A. Roberts, in the 1930s. John McCrady, born in Mississippi in 1911, had already earned national attention in the 1930s. After a New York exhibit in 1937, *Time* magazine described McCrady as "a star risen from the bayous who will do for painting in the South what Faulkner is doing for literature."

McCrady's national reputation did not stop Roberts from requiring the artist to redo his work, according to a 1947 *Mobile Press-Register* story about the hotel.

Roberts ordered the first version taken down and repainted. When McCrady asked why, he was told to do a version in which the Confederates were winning. It was completed by McCrady in 1941.

While two of the four Confederate ships were captured in the battle and one was run aground and destroyed, the scene depicts the engagement before any Southern vessels were damaged at the moment when the most modern ship in the U.S. Navy was sunk.

The painting hung in the Grand Hotel for four decades. When the hotel went through some remodeling in 1985, the painting was donated. It has remained on public display in Foley, Alabama.

The Birdcage Lounge

The lounge at the Grand Hotel didn't have a designated name . . . it was just called "the lounge." Al Agee, Jr., remembers that when J. K. McLean purchased the hotel in the mid-1960s, the employees were asked for suggestions for a name for the lounge. The various departments then voted . . . and the "Birdcage Lounge" became its official name. Some say it was due to the shape. To carry out the theme of the Birdcage Lounge, about six small birdcages with artificial birds were hung throughout the lounge. It was renamed "Bucky's Birdcage Lounge" in 2002 to honor Bucky Miller, who had worked at the Grand Hotel for sixty-one years.

BUCKY'S
Birdcage Lounge

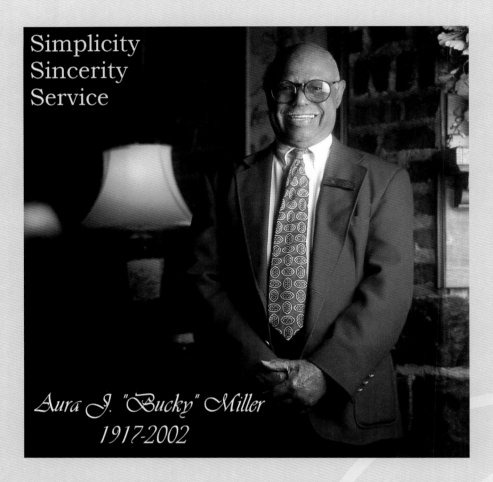

Simplicity
Sincerity
Service

Aura J. "Bucky" Miller
1917-2002

     Aura J. "Bucky" Miller, longtime hospitality ambassador at the Marriott's Grand Hotel, died Friday, August 30, 2002, of complications from diabetes. He was eighty-three years old.

     Bucky began his career at the Grand on April 18, 1941, the first day the hotel reopened, and became a fixture at the resort, where he greeted guests with a hearty, booming welcome. He developed a renowned ability to remember names and regularly surprised guests with a personalized greeting upon their return.

     Bucky was a legend in the hospitality industry, having been honored by the Marriott Corporation with the J. W. Marriott Award of Excellence. The United States Congress and seven Southern states have passed resolutions honoring him. In 2002, the Alabama Department of Tourism recognized Miller as one of Alabama's Unforgettable Faces.

     Bucky served as bartender and server for the majority of his career in the Birdcage Lounge; for the last twelve years he was the hotel's hospitality ambassador, meeting and greeting guests. He became such a familiar figure to guests that the resort renamed its lounge in his honor. It's now Bucky's Birdcage Lounge.

TWELVE COMMANDMENTS FOR PEOPLE WHO WORK WITH PEOPLE

(BUCKY MILLER'S RULES TO LIVE BY)

1. *Love people.*

2. *SMILE.*

3. *Fill the "bucket" of others. Talk to them in such a way as to increase their self-esteem.*

4. *Exhibit a spirit of caring.*

5. *Display a "**Can Do**" attitude.*

6. *Beware! The "**Chicken Little Syndrome**" is contagious.*

7. *Strive for quality in all you do.*

8. *Help people more; hassle people less.*

9. *Never be afraid to try to make things better.*

10. *Train your ears and tame your tongue.*

11. *Tell the truth. It's a lot easier to remember.*

12. **Practice the Golden Rule.**

BUCKY'S MINT JULEP

3 mint leaves
2 tablespoons Simple Syrup (at right)
1 3/4 ounces bourbon
(tested with Maker's Mark or
Walker's Deluxe)
Crushed ice
Maraschino cherry and mint leaf
sprinkled with confectioners' sugar,
for garnish

Place three mint leaves in a silver
julep cup or glass and add the Simple
Syrup. Muddle lightly until the mint
gives off its aroma. Add the bourbon
and mix gently. Fill the glass with
crushed ice. Garnish with a cherry and
an additional mint leaf sprinkled with
confectioners' sugar.

Serves 1

THE ULTIMATE GRAND COCKTAIL FORMULA

The following formula is essential for a hand-crafted, well-balanced cocktail made with absolutely fresh ingredients. Used correctly, this formula can turn a common drink into a world-class cocktail!

3/4 part sour
1 part sweet
1 1/2 parts strong (spirits)

Example for a Whiskey Sour cocktail
Getting prepared

Sour
Cut a lemon into six equal parts (wedges).
Place three wedges in the shaker and muddle.
This will produce the desired 3/4 ounce of juice.

Sweet
Simple Syrup (the cold method)
The goal is to create simple syrup with the exact 50 percent
water to sugar ratio that is technically known as 50 brix.
Fill a container with exactly equal parts
of sugar to *cold water.
Cover the container and shake until the sugar is dissolved.
The syrup will be cloudy at first but will eventually clarify.
Give it one last shake before use.
This procedure may take up to 40 seconds.
Utilize 1 ounce per cocktail and store the rest.

Strong
Pour 1 1/2 ounces of your desired whiskey.

Crafting the cocktail
Fill shaker three-fourths full with ice.
Add 3/4 ounce of fresh juice, 1 ounce of simple syrup and
1 1/2 ounces of whiskey.
**Shake for 12 seconds.
Pour into a rocks glass.
Garnish with a cherry and a slice of orange.

*Use cold water instead of hot water.
Hot water will evaporate and will yield a higher brix, thus
creating a sweeter, unbalanced cocktail.
**This action is done in an arc extending from
the midsection to the side of the head.

EASTER

The air is starting to warm, the flowers have just peeked out of their buds, and the kids are anxiously awaiting their first time in the amazing feature pool for the season. Spring is finally here! Easter marks the beginning of a very exciting time at the Grand. Every year the hotel welcomes back families who have made the Grand their favorite gathering place for the Easter holidays. Peter Cottontail has carefully placed his ten thousand Easter eggs all over our lagoon area, and the kids fill their baskets with oodles of colorful eggs. Afterwards, hundreds of families enjoy the expansive Easter buffet that is presented in both the dining room and our Grand Ballroom. After filling their bellies, the kids all head to the pool and beach to enjoy the live music, fun, and social opportunities. To ensure the kiddos have a good night's sleep, the Grand Hotel sends the Easter Bunny to their rooms for the traditional "bunny tuck-in."

CINNAMON BUN FRENCH TOAST

5 eggs (1 cup)
1 cup half-and-half
1/2 cup sugar
1/4 cup spiced rum
2 tablespoons vanilla extract

2 teaspoons cinnamon
20 cinnamon buns
Confectioners' sugar, fruit and
  mint sprigs, for garnish

Combine the eggs, half-and-half, sugar, spiced rum, vanilla and cinnamon in a shallow dish; whisk until smooth. Dip the buns one at a time into the mixture, coating well. Place on a buttered griddle and cook until golden brown on both sides. Place on serving plates and garnish with confectioners' sugar, fruit and mint sprigs. You may substitute twenty slices Texas toast or French baguette for the cinnamon rolls, if desired.

Serves 10

LOADED DROP BISCUITS

2 cups all-purpose flour
1 tablespoon baking powder
1/2 teaspoon salt
1/3 cup shortening
3/4 cup buttermilk

1/2 cup sour cream
2/3 cup chopped cooked bacon
2/3 cup shredded Cheddar cheese
1/3 cup chopped chives

Mix the flour, baking powder and salt in a bowl. Cut in the shortening with a pastry blender or kitchen knives until the mixture resembles coarse crumbs. Add the buttermilk, sour cream, bacon, cheese and chives and mix just until moistened.

Drop by heaping tablespoonfuls onto a lightly greased baking sheet. Bake in a preheated 425-degree oven for 12 minutes or until light brown.

Makes 18

GRAND SMOOTHIE DUO

Strawberry-Kiwi Smoothie	Mango-Vanilla-Mint Smoothie
2/3 cup strawberries	1 cup chopped mango
1 kiwifruit	1 cup yogurt
1 cup yogurt	2 or 3 mint leaves (optional)
1/2 cup ice	1 teaspoon vanilla extract
	1/2 cup ice

For the strawberry-kiwi smoothie, combine the strawberries, peeled kiwifruit, yogurt and ice in a blender and process until smooth. Pour into a small pitcher. Serve as is or in the Grand Smoothie Duo.

For the mango-vanilla-mint smoothie, combine the mango, yogurt, mint leaves, vanilla and ice in a blender and process until smooth. Pour into a small pitcher. Serve as is or in the Grand Smoothie Duo.

For the Grand Smoothie Duo, pour both mixtures carefully down the sides of glasses at the same time, mixing as little as possible.

Serves 10

STRAWBERRIES ROMANOFF

3 tablespoons butter
7 cups quartered strawberries
1 cup sugar
1/4 cup orange liqueur
(tested with Grand Marnier)

3/4 cup orange juice
1 teaspoon vanilla extract
Vanilla ice cream
Mint leaves, for garnish

Heat a sauté pan over medium heat. Add the butter and strawberries and sauté for 1 to 2 minutes. Add the sugar and sauté for 1 minute. Add the liqueur and ignite, stirring until the flames subside.

Stir in the orange juice and vanilla. Cook until thickened to the desired consistency. Spoon into cocktail glasses and top each serving with a scoop of vanilla ice cream. Garnish with mint leaves.

Serves 10

CRÈME BRÛLÉE

8 egg yolks
1 cup granulated sugar
1 cup milk
1 vanilla bean, split

3 cups heavy cream
1 teaspoon vanilla extract
1/2 cup raw sugar

Combine the egg yolks and granulated sugar in a large bowl and mix well. Bring the milk and vanilla bean to a boil in a saucepan; remove the vanilla bean. Add the hot milk gradually to the egg yolk mixture, whisking constantly. Whisk in the cream and vanilla extract. Let stand for 1 hour to cool.

Spoon into ten baking ramekins and place in a large pan filled halfway with hot water. Cover the pan and bake in a preheated 350-degree oven for 35 to 40 minutes or until the custards are firm around the edges.

Sprinkle the custards with the raw sugar. Caramelize the sugar with a kitchen torch to form a crisp sugar topping. Serve at room temperature.

Serves 10

THE HOTEL OWNERSHIP

Mr. F. H. Chamberlain built the second Grand Hotel in 1847 after the first hotel was destroyed by fire. It was a rambling two-story building with forty rooms. A separate building included the dining room and kitchen, along with another building, which was the bar named "The Texas."

In the 1870s, Captain H. C. Baldwin purchased the hotel. He used some of the old foundations and extended it to three hundred feet in length with sixty suites. Rumor has it that four trips around the porch would equal a mile.

Major James K. Glennon of Mobile purchased the hotel in 1901. His purchase included the Gunnison House and 250 acres of land.

In 1939, Mr. E. A. Roberts purchased the hotel with an additional twenty-five acres. The third Grand Hotel began to evolve. After World War II, Mr. Roberts' company (Waterman Steamship) took over.

Southern Industries bought out Waterman Steamship in 1955.

In 1966, James K. McLean purchased the hotel. He added the current Bay House. The hotel had grown to 172 guest rooms.

Marriott Corporation bought the Grand Hotel in 1981. Shortly after, the North Bay House and the marina building were added, bringing total guest rooms to 306.

In 1999, the Grand Hotel was purchased by the Alabama Real Estate Holdings (now Point Clear Holdings), which is owned by the Retirement Systems of Alabama. During the next few years, the spa building was added, both golf courses were fully renovated, and an extensive property-wide renovation was done after Hurricane Katrina.

Today's Grand Hotel has 405 rooms, including thirty-six suites.

…The Hotel stands within a beautiful crescent, fronting directly on the ocean, and receives the sea breeze unobstructed…

Dr. J.C. Nott
20th, March 20, 1858

BATTLE HOUSE,
MOBILE, ALA.

POINT CLEAR HOTEL,
EASTERN SHORE, MOBILE BAY.

THE subscribers beg leave to return thanks to their friends and the customers of the above named HOTELS, for their kind and liberal patronage, and assure them of their continued desire to study their comfort.

THE POINT CLEAR HOTEL will be opened for Company the latter part of June. The Buildings which will comfortably accommodate THREE HUNDRED PERSONS, are being put in thorough repair; and during the past winter, the grounds and walks have been greatly improved.

POINT CLEAR possesses superior advantages as a place of Summer resort, having a free and unobstructed Gulf breeze, and the most convenient, safe and pure SALT WATER BATHING upon the whole coast. Excellent FISH and OYSTERS are very abundant, and facilities for all aquatic recreations.

☞ A good COTILLION BAND is secured, and every amusement usual at WATERING PLACES will be furnished.

Good Stable accommodations are provided sufficient for twenty horses; and the roads extending upon the high land in every direction, are beautifully shaded with Magnolias, Oaks, Cedar, Pines, &c., &c.

A splendid low pressure Boat, called the "CRESCENT," has been built for this trade the past season, and will ply regularly between Mobile and Point Clear, leaving Mobile EVERY AFTERNOON; and on SUNDAYS, MONDAYS and THURSDAYS, will go down at 10 o'clock A. M., to accommodate those who arrive in Mobile by the morning Boats.

Should this schedule be changed, notice will be given in the Mobile and New Orleans papers.

F. H. CHAMBERLAIN & CO.,
PROPRIETORS.

MOBILE, May 25th, 1858.

LETTER FROM DR. J. C. NOTT.

NEW ORLEANS, 20th March, 1858.

*Gentlemen:—*I take much pleasure in bearing witness to the merits of Point Clear as a summer resort, and have no hesitation in giving it a decided preference over any Watering place with which I am acquainted on the Gulf of Mexico. The Hotel stands within a beautiful crescent, fronting directly on the ocean, and receives the sea breeze unobstructed. The Salt bathing is less than one hundred paces from the Hotel door; the drinking water is supplied by pure springs from the pine hills in the rear, and the healthfulness of the position has been fairly tested by a long series of years. It escaped entirely, even the terrible epidemic of 1853 which ravaged the coast from Rio de Janeiro to Norfolk, to say nothing of less trying years. I have been in the habit of visiting Point Clear almost every summer.

J. C. NOTT.

Professor of Anatomy in University of Louisiana.

To Messrs. CHAMBERLAIN & DARLING.

POINT CLEAR HOTEL BOUGHT BY NEW CORP.

$35,000 Paid for Property; Extensive Improvement Being Planned

Sale of the historic Point Clear Hotel on Mobile Bay's eastern shore by the James K. Glennon estate to the Grand Hotel Corporation is announced.

The corporation paid the estate $35,000 for the property—the building, and 700 feet of bay frontage running from just west of the Glennon cottage to a point 100 feet north of Point Clear Creek.

An extensive improvement of the hotel and the grounds, including new bulkheading along the shore, is planned, it was learned.

In corporation papers for the Grand Hotel Corporation were filed in probate court today by Marion R. Vickers, an attorney. The authorized capital stock is $100,000, and of this, $40,000 has been paid in.

President of the corporation, with $38,000 of the stock, is E. A. Hirs, who is traveling auditor for the Waterman Steamship Corporation. Vice president is L. M. Torbert, secretary to the president of Waterman's with $1,000 worth of shares, and Katherine Gray, who is Vickers' secretary, is secretary of the company, and also holds $1,000 worth of stock. These three also compose the directorate.

Will Assume Old Name

The Point Clear Hotel was now years ago as the Grand Hotel, and it was understood that it will again assume that name. Mat Thorner, trustee of the Glennon estate, said his records did not know when the original hotel was built, but he produced a drawing of it, made in 1854. The first building was destroyed by fire, and the long, two-stories hotel that now stands on Great Point Clear was built in the latter part of the nineteenth century.

Heirs of the Glennon estate are: Katherine G. Manorner, Agnes G. ..er, John F. Glennon, James H. ..o, Harry McDonnell, James McDonnell, Julian B. McDonnell, Alfred N. McDonnell, Paul A. McDonnell, and Owen E. McDonnell all of Mobile and William McDonnell of Sheffield, Ala.

The estate retains ownership of the remainder of its 200-acre holding at the Point, including the cottages and land running north...

*1949 Schedule of Rates
and Recreational Facilities*

Recreational Facilities at the
GRAND HOTEL
★ ★ ★

18-Hole Golf Course
Tennis - Shuffleboard - Cycling
Fishing — Bay, Gulf, or Inland
Hunting (In Season)
Bathing — Fresh Water Pool or
Bay Swimming (Sandy Beach)
Children's Playground
Children's Playhouse
Motor and Sail Boats
Riding Horses

Grand Hotel

"Relax and Play on Mobile Bay"

POINT CLEAR, ALABAMA

OPEN ALL YEAR

SCHEDULE OF RATES
APRIL 1ST. 1949

Grand Hotel
POINT CLEAR, ALABAMA

EUROPEAN PLAN
RATES

East and West Wing	Double	11.00
East and West Wing Suites	Double	16.00
North Wing	Double	11.00
North Wing Suites	Double	16.00
	Extra Person	4.00

Any child occupying a separate room will be charged full rate.

Breakfast — Club breakfast	$ .70 up, also a la carte
Luncheon— Regular luncheon	$1.50, also a la carte
Dinner — Regular dinner	$2.50 up, also a la carte

Limousine Service — To or from Mobile, $3.50 per person
Limousine Service — To or from Airport, 5.00 per person

THE SPA AT THE GRAND

Bathed in the charm and beauty of the South and serenaded by the timeless rhythm of the sea, the Spa at the Grand Hotel invites you to step into a world of gracious hospitality and luxurious service. Our pleasure is to create for you an unforgettable spa experience in a serene environment designed to relax, revitalize, and rejuvenate the mind, the body, and the spirit. Experience such wonderful healing rituals as warm stone massage, color light and marine bathing therapies, aromatherapy, and a wide range of customized skin care and body services. Visit our beautiful salon for the latest in hair design, makeup, bridal services, and, of course, the very best in nail care, all customized to your needs so that you leave us looking and feeling your best!

If you still want more, discover what's new in fitness and rev up your energy on our state-of-the-art cardio and strength equipment! Complete your visit with a stop at our inviting spa boutique. Shop for unusual one-of-a-kind items to remind you of your stay, or just linger over a drink and watch the boats nestled in our marina. We are devoted to your complete well-being and take pride in attending to your personal needs and preferences. Allow yourself to drift gently with us for an hour, for a day, or for a week, as we take you on the ultimate sensory journey to renewed energy, joy, and health. Imagine the possibilities . . . . .

MOTHER'S DAY

Honor your mother with another family tradition at the Grand Hotel. You can start with an early morning massage at our spa and then spoil her with a beautifully presented buffet in either the Grand Dining Room or Grand Ballroom. The Grand Hotel chefs create ice carving masterpieces ranging from intricate swans to ice baskets filled with colorful flowers. After filling up with delicious desserts and scrumptious fresh seafood items, mothers enjoy a relaxing stroll through the hotel grounds, which are in luscious bloom during the month of May.

The Grand Southern Belle

Experience a truly magical day! Begin in Neptune's Hideaway with a luxurious body polish to exfoliate and restore luster to your skin. Next, a creamy, wonderfully aromatic body mask of French clays, essential oils, and papaya is applied, followed by gentle steam and a cascade of warm showers pulsating over your entire body. Follow this with a fifty-minute massage and a fifty-minute signature European facial. Indulge in the Grand Spa pedicure and Grand Spa manicure. Then finish with a shampoo and blow-dry and full makeup application. A Spa Cuisine luncheon will be served.

Simply stated… Life is Grand!

BISCUITS

3 cups cake flour, sifted
1 tablespoon baking powder
1 tablespoon sugar
1 teaspoon salt
$^1/_3$ cup shortening

$^1/_3$ cup butter, chilled and cut
into $^1/_2$-inch cubes
1 cup buttermilk
Melted butter for brushing

Combine the cake flour, baking powder, sugar and salt in a mixing bowl. Add the shortening and mix at low speed until combined. Add $^1/_3$ cup butter and mix just until coarse crumbs form; do not overmix. Add the buttermilk gradually, mixing until moistened.

Roll 1 inch thick on a floured surface. Cut with a plain round cutter; do not twist the cutter as it may prevent the biscuits from rising completely. Arrange on a baking sheet lined with baking parchment.

Brush the biscuits with melted butter. Bake in a preheated 375-degree oven for 20 to 25 minutes or until fluffy and golden brown. You can also bake in a convection oven at 325 degrees.

Makes 20

HONEY PECAN CHICKEN SALAD

4 cups finely chopped roasted chicken
$^3/_4$ cup finely chopped onion
$^3/_4$ cup finely chopped celery
$^1/_2$ cup toasted pecan pieces

$1^1/_2$ cups mayonnaise
$^1/_2$ cup honey
2 tablespoons Dijon mustard
Salt and pepper to taste

Combine the chicken with the onion, celery and pecans in a bowl and mix well. Add the mayonnaise, honey and Dijon mustard and toss to coat evenly. Season with salt and pepper.

Serves 10

Grand Hotel

Meetings and retreats at the Grand Hotel Resort have become a tradition for many businesses and groups around the country. With 39,000 square feet of meeting space indoors, the Grand Hotel also has many beautiful outdoor areas for a reception or ceremony. Two of the Grand Hotel's most loyal groups are the Alabama Funeral Directors Association and the Southern Radiology Conference; they have been coming to the Grand Hotel for over fifty years.

Jack & I first went to the Grand Hotel in 1952 on our honeymoon—actually on our way to Sea Island, Georgia. Sea Island was lively & fun for young people <u>but</u> it was to the Grand Hotel that we returned year after year for all these years.

Tho we traveled the world, we probably haven't missed more than 2 or 3 years spending summers at the Grand. You might say "It's like coming home".

Our children love it (because they grew up here) & their children love it. There is nothing like the slow pace, friendly people & beautiful surroundings to stamp an indelible print in your heart.

Jack always said he knew heaven was going to be like the golf course at Lakewood. I'd love to be able to ask him. I'm sure he was right.

See you this summer!

a very happy guest,
Bette King

MEMORIAL DAY

Summer starts early at the Grand Hotel. To the staff and guests, Memorial Day officially begins the summer season. The Southern hospitality of the Grand Hotel provides the perfect Memorial Day background with its rich historical significance. Generations of families have been spending Memorial Day swimming, golfing, fishing, dining, or just relaxing with a mint julep from Bucky's Birdcage Lounge.

Grand Hotel Boat

The Grand Hotel boat was operated out of the marina throughout the 1950s and 1960s. Archie Denton was the boat captain during these years and learned the hot spots for catching Bay fish, including flounder, speckled trout, and redfish. Many guests learned to fish on Mobile Bay, either simply from our pier using a cane pole or on a chartered bay boat. Our pier continues to be a hot spot with bait and cane poles provided for hotel guests to use at their leisure.

BAY BOATS—MOBILE BAY

Beginning in the early nineteenth century, shallow-draft boats provided transportation and a connection between Mobile and the Eastern Shore, including the Grand Hotel at Point Clear. The boats were first powered by sail and later by steam—names like the *Pleasure Bay*, *Annie*, the *Crescent*, the *Bay Queen*, the *Magnolia*, the *Apollo*, and *Ocean Wave* coursed the waters of Mobile Bay. Daily service was provided to and from the Eastern Shore; the fare was twenty-five to fifty cents. Stories abound of romantic encounters, gaiety, and music on the decks, as the bay boats arrived at the docks at the wharves along the Eastern Shore, delivering passengers to their destinations.

These bay excursions seem glamorous today, but the treks across the bay could also be dangerous, with fire and storms posing the biggest threats. Many of the bay boats, and the wharves where they docked, met their fate during the hurricanes of 1906 and 1916.

The auto age—in 1927 the Cochrane Bridge was opened, completing the causeway, crossing the north end of Mobile Bay—opened up road transportation between Mobile and the Eastern Shore, eliminating the need for the bay boats. Passengers and deliveries of goods could now be transported the entire length of the journey by car or truck. Bay boats were no longer feasible, hence the end of this seemingly romantic era.

WORLD WAR II

During World War II, the Grand Hotel was the focal point for "Operation Ivory Soap" training. Colonel Thompson contacted the then-owner, Mr. Strat White-Spunner, and used the hotel as his base of operations. As a donation to the war effort, Mr. Roberts turned the Grand Hotel and its facilities over to the U.S. Army Air Force to be used as its maritime training school. Basic seamanship, marine, and aquatic training for the Army officers and men of the aircraft repair and maintenance units was held at the Grand Hotel. Operation Ivory Soap training began on July 10, 1944.

Using the Grand Hotel, officers and enlisted men moved in and began living in "Navy style." All personnel referred to the floors as decks, kept time by a ship's bell, and indulged in the use of tobacco only when the "smoking lamp" was lit. The courses included swimming, special calisthenics, marching, drill, navigation, ship identification, signaling, cargo handling, ship orientation, sail making, amphibious operations, and more. Two men from each ship were also trained to be underwater divers.

During a five-month period, the school turned out five thousand highly trained Air Force seamen. Afterwards, the men and their ships went to war, as did Colonel Thompson. The men of Operation Ivory Soap participated in the landings in the Philippines, Guam, Tinian, Saipan, Iwo Jima, and Okinawa. Fighter aircraft and B-29s took off from the bases and flew continuous missions over Japan. The men who trained at the Grand Hotel were instrumental in saving many lives, as well as aircraft.

THE MARINA

The Grand Hotel Marina is located north of the hotel and west of Scenic 98. The marina was originally a part of the Lakewood swamps. Over time the area was dredged, bulkheads installed, and slips completed. Point Clear Creek empties into the marina so there is a natural flow of water through the marina and empties into Mobile Bay. There are reports of steamships in the late 1800s traveling from Mobile to the Grand to transport passengers who had gone to Mobile to see a show. For example, in 1946 the Alabama State Dock's yacht transported hotel guests between Mobile and the Grand. The play *John Brown's Body*, starring Anne Baxter, Joseph Cotten, and Tyrone Power, was in Mobile, so a number of the guests would travel by boat from the marina to Mobile to see the play. Today the marina has thirty-six slips. We have added fueling for both diesel and marine fuel. All of the slips have electrical, water, and cable TV hook-ups. The marina has been and will continue to be a key feature of The Grand Hotel Marriott Resort, Golf Club, and Spa.

HAPPILY EVER AFTER...

Once upon a time there were a bride, a groom, and an oak tree. What starts as a backdrop becomes an integral part of the memories that last a lifetime.

The Grand Hotel becomes a major character in a storybook wedding, as it has been a host for generations. We have seen grandmothers, mothers, and daughters married on the same lawn.

Many couples return year after year with their children, grandchildren, and great-grandchildren to watch the same breathtaking Mobile Bay sunset they watched more than fifty years ago on their wedding day.

SHRIMP AND GRITS

80 (16- to 20-count) peeled shrimp
1/2 cup Cajun seasoning
1/3 cup olive oil
2 tablespoons lemon juice
2 tablespoons brandy
2 tablespoons wine
2 tablespoons minced garlic
2 tablespoons minced shallots

2 tablespoons butter
2 tablespoons Cajun seasoning
1/4 cup white wine
4 cups cooked grits
2 cups (8 ounces) shredded
    Cheddar cheese
3 tablespoons chopped cilantro
2 1/2 cups Cajun Cream Sauce (below)

Combine the shrimp with 1/2 cup Cajun seasoning, the olive oil, lemon juice, brandy and 2 tablespoons wine in a sealable plastic bag, turning to coat evenly. Marinate in the refrigerator for 3 hours or longer.

Sauté the garlic and shallots in the butter in a saucepan. Add 2 tablespoons Cajun seasoning and 1/4 cup wine. Stir in the grits, cheese and cilantro; mix well. Cook just until heated through; keep warm.

Drain the shrimp and grill or sauté in a cast-iron skillet or sauté pan until pink and cooked through. Serve with the grits and the Cajun Cream Sauce.

Serves 10

CAJUN CREAM SAUCE

1 tablespoon chopped garlic
1 tablespoon chopped shallot
Olive oil for sautéing
1/4 cup brandy

2 cups heavy cream
2 tablespoons Cajun seasoning
2 cups Lobster Bisque (page 50)
Salt and pepper to taste

Sauté the garlic and shallot in a small amount of olive oil in a saucepan. Add the brandy and stir to loosen the brown bits from the saucepan. Stir in the cream and Cajun seasoning and cook until reduced by one-third. Add the Lobster Bisque and cook until reduced to the desired creamy consistency. Season with salt and pepper.

Serves 10

CRAB DIP

24 ounces cream cheese, softened
3/4 cup mayonnaise
6 tablespoons sherry
2 tablespoons Dijon mustard
8 ounces crab meat
2/3 cup chopped sun-dried
 tomatoes, reconstituted

2 tablespoons minced shallots
Salt, black pepper and cayenne pepper
 to taste
Tri-colored tortillas or pita chips
Vegetable oil for frying

Combine the cream cheese, mayonnaise, sherry and Dijon mustard in a food processor and mix until smooth. Add the crab meat, sun-dried tomatoes and shallots. Season with salt, black pepper and cayenne pepper. Process until well mixed. Spoon into a serving bowl.

Cut tri-colored tortillas into wedges. Fry in vegetable oil in a saucepan until crisp; drain on paper towels. Serve with the dip.

Serves 10

ROSE PETAL AND VANILLA SORBET

3 cups plain yogurt
1/2 cup rose petals
3 egg whites

2/3 cup sugar
1 vanilla bean
1/4 cup brandy

Combine the yogurt and rose petals in a blender and process until the rose petals are finely chopped and well mixed. Pour into a large bowl.

Combine the egg whites and sugar in a mixing bowl and beat until very soft peaks form. Fold into the yogurt mixture.

Split the vanilla bean and combine with the brandy in a saucepan. Bring to a simmer and simmer for 5 minutes. Scrape the seeds from the vanilla pod into the brandy with a paring knife and discard the pod. Fold into the yogurt mixture.

Spoon into an ice cream maker and freeze using the manufacturer's directions.

Serves 10

Dancing Under the Stars

"Dancing Under the Stars" was a longtime tradition at the Grand Hotel. It was held on the bay at Julep Point every Thursday and Saturday. Hotel guests, local residents, and even people from Mobile would come out for cocktails and dancing to the sounds of groups such as the Jack Normand Band. Dancing studios would also bring students out to help them practice in front of a live band. This tradition ended in the late eighties, but is still remembered by many endearing guests.

RESORT ACTIVITIES

Resort activities have a long and important history at the Grand Hotel Marriott Resort, Golf Club, and Spa. Back when the Grand Hotel originally opened, there was always a focus on activities for the children along with the adults. We continue that tradition today. Some of the oldest photos we have are of our guests sailing on Mobile Bay with the Grand in the background.

Today, resort activities have grown to include the Teen Center, Fun Camp, bicycles, putting green, croquet court, horseshoe pits, and a private beach for sailing and other watercraft. During holidays the resort features special events. For example, on the Fourth of July we have our own Grand fireworks display. We also feature special visitors who tuck in our youngest guests: reindeer tuck-in during Christmas, turkey tuck-in during Thanksgiving, bunny tuck-in during Easter, and Uncle Sam tuck-in on the Fourth of July.

During the summer months we offer a dive-in movie at the outdoor pool, which is very popular with our youngest guests. What could be better than playing in the pool on a hot summer night but enjoying a hit movie at the same time? When you talk to our guests, the things they remember are all of the activities that we have for guests of all ages.

Windy Johnston

A favorite to all children who visited the Grand Hotel from 1950 until the mid-1980s, Windy Johnston was the one who kept them entertained. As the recreation director, he was responsible for training all the lifeguards for both the pool and the beach and teaching children how to swim and sail. He also helped to oversee the pier facilities, sailboats, water skiing, bicycles, and the holiday and children's activities program. There was hardly a guest who did not recognize him as he whizzed around the hotel grounds on his bicycle wearing the perennial red cap and swim trunks. He truly was a "bay rat" who never wore socks, and it was rare that he would be wearing shoes. The famous Fourth of July Grand Hotel regatta was started in the 1960s under Windy's direction.

THE GRAND POOL

The Grand Hotel pool has been a summer tradition for hotel guests and Lakewood members alike. The original pool was located directly off the marina waters. It was a popular spot and hosted many family vacations, along with swim competitions. It was a large pool with separate children and adult areas. The bar that was situated alongside the pool was called the Pavilion. The poolside grill was named the Pelican's Nest.

Today, the Grand Hotel pool is bigger and better than ever. The pool was moved to the former location of the cottages, in between the North Bay House and the marina building. A bar called the Marlin Bar was built, and a poolside grill that kept the name the Pelican's Nest. The new pool added many features, such as a waterfall in the kids' area that is at the bottom of the long Grand Hotel pool slide. There is also a separate adult area you have to be twenty-one years of age to enter. Beautiful libations, refreshments, and grilled treats are forever being served to tanning guests during the summer months at the Grand Hotel.

"Life is Grand"

104

GRAND HOTEL LEMONADE

2 lemons
1/4 teaspoon Simple Syrup (see page 67)
Water and crushed ice

Cut one lemon into thin slices. Squeeze the juice of the second lemon into a 12-ounce glass. Add the Simple Syrup and enough water and crushed ice to fill the glass. Arrange the lemon slices down the side of the glass in a decorative pattern. You can also prepare this by simply adding the halves of the squeezed lemon to the glass and garnishing it with a lemon wedge.

Serves 1

WEST INDIES SALAD

12 ounces crab meat	Salt and pepper to taste
1/4 cup finely chopped onion	1/3 cup mixed finely chopped green, red
1/4 cup apple cider vinegar	and yellow bell peppers
1/4 cup vegetable oil	Micro greens, for garnish

Mix the crab meat and onion in a bowl. Combine the cider vinegar, oil, salt and pepper in a bowl and mix well. Add to the crab meat and mix gently. Cover the mixture completely with crushed ice.

Let stand in the refrigerator for 24 hours.

Drain the crab meat mixture well. Add the bell peppers and mix gently. Spoon into molds, pressing down to pack well. Unmold onto serving plates and garnish with micro greens.

Serves 4

JUBILEE

When it will happen nobody knows . . . why it happens even the experts aren't sure. Only this is certain: The cry of "Jubilee!" up and down the beach on the Eastern Shore of Mobile Bay means thrilling excitement, fun, and seafood for all.

Among its other distinctions Point Clear may be called "the Jubilee Center of the World" because the phenomenon occurs within six or eight miles up and down the beach from here—and nowhere else as far as we know.

Our guests ask more questions about Jubilees than any other single subject, so we've prepared the following to explain, as best we can.

In a Jubilee, thousands of fish and/or crabs and/or shrimp come right up on shore.

The folks who quickly gather after the first cry of "Jubilee!" have no trouble at all filling buckets, sacks, and even washtubs with the high-priced delicacies of the deep. ●➤

Despite the inconvenient hour—Jubilees happen at night, often between midnight and dawn—it takes no time at all for a crowd to gather. The shoreline rings with shouts and laughter and squeals of excitement, and informality is the rule.

On some occasions it's primarily flounders that congregate and at other times it's a "shrimp Jubilee" or "crab Jubilee"—but generally all three species plus a few other fish and eels are involved.

Jubilees have not been positively explained by science but two theories exist, both based upon changing bay water. Since Mobile Bay is fed by rivers, some believe the fish and shellfish may be dazed by a sudden merging of fresh and salt water. Others believe it's caused by the changing temperature of the water following heavy rains.

But no participant in a Jubilee ever stopped to ponder the questions, which is just as well. It wouldn't be nearly as much fun if all the mystery were explained away!

No one knows when or at what area on the beach the next Jubilee will occur. Most summers there are several, but you can't even be sure of that!

JUBILEE MARY

1 lime, cut into halves	Dash of pepper
Cajun seasoning	$1/4$ cup tomato juice
1 rib celery	$1/4$ cup vegetable juice cocktail
$1/2$ jalapeño chile	(tested with V-8)
1 tablespoon fresh lime juice	$1^1/2$ ounces pepper vodka
1 tablespoon fresh lemon juice	(tested with Absolut)
$1/2$ tablespoon Worcestershire sauce	Lemon wedge, celery rib, olives and
Dash of garlic salt	Cajun-seasoned broiled shrimp,
Dash of salt	for garnish

Squeeze the juice of one lime onto a small plate. Sprinkle Cajun seasoning into a second small plate. Dip the rim of a hurricane glass into the lime juice and then into the seasoning to rim the glass.

Combine one celery rib, the jalapeño chile, 1 tablespoon lime juice, the lemon juice, Worcestershire sauce, garlic salt, salt and pepper in a blender. Process until smooth. Pour carefully into the prepared glass.

Add the tomato juice, vegetable juice cocktail and vodka; mix well. Add ice and garnish with a lemon wedge, an additional celery rib, olives and Cajun-seasoned broiled shrimp

Serves 1

SALTWATER GRILL

Only one word should be used when describing the experience that guests have when dining in the Saltwater Grill . . . amazing, upbeat, unique, casual, and entertaining! Opened in 2006, the Saltwater Grill is the newest addition to the Grand Hotel restaurant portfolio. The Saltwater Grill was designed to fill the need of the casual guest who might dine in the restaurant numerous times during the week with friends and family. "20 Entrées under $20" makes frequent dining possible. Fresh local seafood is featured daily through the "Fresh Catch of the Day" and Saltwater specialty items such as Cedar Plank Redfish or Coconut Shrimp. The Saltwater Grill is a local favorite and has won multiple awards for its Saltwater Signature Crab Cakes and Jubilee Pasta.

Located in the historic main building, the Saltwater Grill boasts the best view of Mobile Bay sunsets. While the children are entertained by croquet, Ping-Pong, and horseshoes, you will find it remarkably easy to relax, unwind, and forget the reason why you needed to relax in the first place. Some of the "luscious libations" that will assist in the relaxation are the Mobile Bay Sunset, Point Clear of Stress, and a Hook, Line and Sinker.

SALTWATER GRILL

CASUAL DINING ON MOBILE BAY

Jubilee Seafood Pasta

JUBILEE SEAFOOD PASTA

30 (16- to 20-count) peeled
  jumbo shrimp
4 cups olive oil
1 cup minced garlic
30 (20- to 30-count) scallops
2 cups crawfish
1 cup julienned red bell pepper
1 cup julienned green bell pepper
1 cup julienned yellow bell pepper
1/2 cup chopped shallots
2 cups julienned red onions

1/3 cup olive oil
2 cups shiitake mushrooms
3 cups spinach
12 ounces green tomatoes, chopped
10 cups cooked pasta
Salt and pepper to taste
1/2 cup brandy
1/2 cup white wine
Cajun Cream Sauce (page 97)
1 cup (4 ounces) shredded Parmesan
  cheese, for garnish

Combine the shrimp with 2 cups olive oil and 1/2 cup garlic in a sealable plastic bag and turn to coat evenly. Combine the scallops with 2 cups olive oil and 1/2 cup garlic in a sealable plastic bag and turn to coat evenly. Marinate in the refrigerator for 1 hour or longer.

Sauté the shrimp and scallops with the crawfish, bell peppers, shallots and onions in 1/3 cup olive oil in a large sauté pan. Add the mushrooms, spinach and green tomatoes and sauté until the spinach is wilted. Add the pasta and season with salt and pepper; mix well.

Add the brandy and wine, stirring to loosen the brown bits from the sauté pan. Stir in the Cajun Cream Sauce and bring to a boil. Spoon into serving bowls and garnish with the cheese.

Serves 10

CORN BREAD

2 cups cornmeal
1 cup all-purpose flour
2 teaspoons baking powder
2$^{1}/_{2}$ cups buttermilk
3 eggs
2 tablespoons bacon drippings
$^{1}/_{3}$ cup honey
$^{1}/_{2}$ cup corn kernels

$^{1}/_{4}$ cup finely chopped red bell pepper
$^{1}/_{4}$ cup finely chopped green bell pepper
2 to 3 tablespoons finely chopped onion,
   or to taste
1 teaspoon minced garlic
$^{1}/_{2}$ cup (2 ounces) shredded
   Cheddar cheese
Bacon drippings for coating

Mix the cornmeal, flour and baking powder in a bowl. Combine the buttermilk and eggs in a mixing bowl and mix well. Add the cornmeal mixture gradually, mixing until smooth. Stir in the honey.

Heat 2 tablespoons bacon drippings in a sauté pan. Add the corn, bell peppers, onion and garlic and sauté for 2 to 3 minutes. Add to the batter with the cheese and mix well.

Spoon the batter into muffin cups coated with additional bacon drippings. Bake in a preheated 350-degree oven for 15 to 20 minutes or until set and golden brown. May bake in a cast-iron skillet if desired.

Makes 10

CAJUN SWORDFISH

$^{1}/_{4}$ cup olive oil
2 tablespoons blackening spice
2 teaspoons minced garlic

20 (3-ounce) portions swordfish
Crawfish Ragoût (page 116)
Cajun Cream Sauce (page 97)

Combine the olive oil, blackening spice and garlic in a sealable plastic bag. Add the swordfish fillets and turn to coat evenly. Marinate in the refrigerator for 3 hours or longer.

Place the fillets on a preheated medium-hot grill at a 45-degree angle. Grill for 1 to 2 minutes. Turn the fish $^{1}/_{4}$ turn to mark the fillets in a diamond pattern and grill for 1 to 2 minutes longer on that side. Turn the fillets over and repeat the grilling process. Spoon Crawfish Ragoût over the swordfish and top with Cajun Cream Sauce.

Serves 10

COCONUT SHRIMP

Ginger Marmalade Sauce
2 tablespoons minced fresh ginger
1 tablespoon minced garlic
2 tablespoons sesame oil
$1^1/2$ cups orange marmalade
2 tablespoons orange liqueur
(tested with Triple Sec)
$1/4$ cup sweet Thai chili sauce
1 cup orange juice

Coconut Shrimp
3 cups all-purpose flour
$2^1/2$ cups panko
$1^1/2$ cups coconut
6 eggs
1 cup coconut milk
70 (16- to 20-count) peeled shrimp
Vegetable oil for deep-frying

For the sauce, sauté the ginger and garlic in the sesame oil in a saucepan for 1 minute. Stir in the marmalade. Add the liqueur, stirring to loosen the brown bits from the saucepan. Stir in the chili sauce and orange juice. Bring to a boil and cook until the sauce has the desired consistency.

For the shrimp, place the flour in a shallow plate. Mix the bread crumbs and coconut in a shallow bowl. Beat the eggs with the coconut milk in a shallow bowl. Dip the shrimp into the flour, then into the egg wash and then into the coconut mixture, coating well; place on baking parchment. Heat vegetable oil to 350 degrees in a deep fryer. Add the shrimp and deep-fry until golden brown. Serve with the sauce.

Serves 10

CRAWFISH RAGOÛT

1 cup crawfish tail meat
$3/4$ cup frozen lima beans, thawed
1 teaspoon minced garlic
1 teaspoon Cajun seasoning
$1/2$ teaspoon filé powder
Olive oil for sautéing

2 tablespoons brandy
2 tablespoons white wine
$3/4$ cup Chowchow (page 117)
2 tablespoons chopped cilantro
Salt and pepper to taste

Sauté the crawfish meat and lima beans with the garlic, Cajun seasoning and filé powder in a small amount of olive oil in a sauté pan. Add the brandy and wine and stir to loosen the brown bits from the sauté pan. Add the Chowchow, cilantro, salt and pepper and sauté for 2 to 3 minutes. Serve over the Cajun Swordfish (page 115).

Serves 10

CHOWCHOW

1 head cabbage, chopped
2 cups chopped onions
2 cups chopped green tomatoes
2 cups chopped green bell peppers
1 cup chopped red bell pepper
3 tablespoons vegetable oil
1 1/2 cups sugar

3 tablespoons salt
1 teaspoon turmeric
2 teaspoons celery seeds
2 1/2 cups vinegar
2 teaspoons dry mustard
1/2 teaspoon ginger

Sauté the cabbage, onions, green tomatoes and bell peppers in the oil in a large saucepan until tender. Add the sugar, salt, turmeric, celery seeds, vinegar, dry mustard and ginger and mix well. Bring to a boil and cook until the liquid completely evaporates. Remove from the heat. Chill immediately until serving time.

Makes about 10 cups

HOLLANDAISE SAUCE

1 1/2 cups (3 sticks) butter
1/3 cup white wine vinegar
1/3 cup white wine
2 tablespoons chopped shallots

6 egg yolks
1 tablespoons lemon juice
Salt and black pepper to taste
Pinch of cayenne pepper

Heat the butter in a saucepan over low heat until the solids sink to the bottom of the saucepan. Pour off the clarified butter on the top, discarding the solids. Cool to lukewarm. Combine the wine vinegar, wine and shallots in a small saucepan. Bring to a low boil and cook until reduced by two-thirds. Strain into a bowl and cool, discarding the solids.

Combine the reduced wine mixture with the egg yolks in a stainless steel bowl; mix well. Place over a saucepan of boiling water over low heat. Cook until the mixture forms a ribbon when the whisk is lifted, whisking constantly; test by seeing if the ribbon will float on top of the mixture. Whisk in the clarified butter very gradually. Season with the lemon juice, salt, black pepper and cayenne pepper. You can hold this sauce in a warm place for up to 3 hours.

Makes about 2 cups

CEDAR-ROASTED REDFISH

Creole Hollandaise Sauce
2¹/2 cups Hollandaise Sauce (page 117)
6 ounces tomatoes, peeled, seeded and
finely chopped
2 tablespoons chopped chives
2 teaspoons Cajun seasoning

Cedar-Roasted Redfish
10 whole redfish, cleaned and
heads removed
Salt and pepper to taste
20 ounces Crab Cake mix (page 136)
Micro greens and Fried Shallot Garnish
(page 33), for garnish

For the sauce, combine the Hollandaise Sauce, tomatoes, chives and Cajun seasoning in a saucepan and heat to serving temperature. Keep warm.

For the redfish, rinse the cavities of the fish and sprinkle with salt and pepper. Spoon the Crab Cake mix into the cavities and press the sides closed. Sear the fish on both sides on a griddle.

Place on heated presoaked cedar planks and roast in a preheated 350-degree oven for 8 to 10 minutes or until cooked through. Serve with the sauce and garnish with micro greens and Fried Shallot Garnish.

Serves 10

FRIED GREEN TOMATOES

All-purpose flour
Cornmeal
Egg wash (egg and water)

20 (¹/3-inch) slices green tomato
Vegetable oil for deep-frying
Salt and pepper to taste

Place flour and cornmeal in separate shallow plates. Place egg wash in a shallow bowl. Dip the tomato slices into flour, then egg wash and then cornmeal; arrange on paper towels.

Heat vegetable oil to 350 degrees in a deep fryer. Deep-fry the tomato slices for 2 to 3 minutes or until golden brown. Drain on paper towels and season with salt and pepper.

Serves 10

PECAN GROUPER

1 cup all-purpose flour
1¹/2 cups panko
1 cup pecan pieces
4 eggs
¹/4 cup (about) milk

10 (7-ounce) grouper fillets
Canola oil for pan-frying
Peach Beurre Blanc (page 123)
Peach Chutney (below)

Place the flour in a shallow dish. Mix the bread crmbs and pecans in a shallow dish. Combine the eggs with enough milk to measure 1 cup. Pour the egg wash into a shallow dish. Dip the fillets in the flour, then the egg wash and then in the pecan mixture, coating evenly.

Heat a small amount of canola oil in a skillet over medium heat. Add the fillets and panfry for 2 to 3 minutes on each side or until cooked through. Serve with Peach Beurre Blanc and Peach Chutney.

Serves 10

PEACH CHUTNEY

1¹/2 pounds (about) peaches,
peeled and chopped
²/3 cup chopped red onion
¹/3 cup chopped red bell pepper
¹/3 cup chopped green bell pepper
¹/3 cup chopped yellow bell pepper

1 tablespoon minced fresh ginger
Butter for sautéing
³/4 cup packed brown sugar
¹/4 cup peach schnapps
1 tablespoon vanilla extract

Sauté the peaches, onion and bell peppers with the ginger in a small amount of butter in a saucepan until tender. Add the brown sugar and cook until caramelized, stirring constantly. Add the schnapps and vanilla, stirring to loosen the brown bits from the saucepan. Simmer for 2 to 3 minutes. Serve with Pecan Grouper (above).

Serves 10

CRAWFISH ÉTOUFFÉE

^{1}/2 cup (1 stick) butter
^{1}/2 cup all-purpose flour
2 cups chopped onions
^{2}/3 cup chopped red bell pepper
^{2}/3 cup chopped green bell pepper
^{2}/3 cup chopped yellow bell pepper
1 cup chopped green onions
1 cup chopped celery
1 tablespoon minced garlic
4 cups crawfish meat
Butter for sautéing

^{1}/2 cup brandy
^{1}/2 cup wine
3 cups canned diced tomatoes
^{1}/3 cup chopped parsley
2 teaspoons Cajun seasoning
Salt and black pepper to taste
^{1}/2 teaspoon cayenne pepper
4 ounces rice, cooked
Frozen puff pastry, thawed
1 egg, beaten

Melt ^{1}/2 cup butter in a small saucepan. Stir in the flour and cook over medium-low heat until golden brown, stirring constantly to form a roux.

Sauté the onions, bell peppers, green onions, celery, garlic and crawfish meat in a small amount of butter in a saucepan until the vegetables are tender. Add the brandy and wine and stir to loosen the brown bits from the saucepan. Stir in the tomatoes, parsley, Cajun seasoning, salt, black pepper and cayenne pepper. Simmer over low heat for 5 minutes. Add the roux and mix well. Cook until thickened.

Spoon the rice into ten oven-proof serving bowls. Spoon the étouffée over the rice.

Cut ten rounds of puff pastry and place one on each serving. Brush with a mixture of the egg and a small amount of water. Bake in a preheated 375-degree oven for 10 to 12 minutes or until golden brown.

Serves 10

HOOK, LINE AND SINKER

1 lemon, cut into halves
Appletini sugar for rimming
$^1/_2$ lime
$1^1/_2$ ounces citrus rum
(tested with Bacardi Limón)

1 ounce blue curaçao
1 ounce Hpnotiq
2 tablespoons Simple Syrup (see page 67)
Crushed ice
Slice of star fruit, for garnish

Squeeze the juice from the lemon onto a shallow plate. Sprinkle Appletini sugar onto a second plate. Dip the rim of a confetti glass into the lemon juice and then into the sugar to coat the rim.

Cut the lime into three wedges and place in a cocktail shaker. Muddle the lime wedges to release about $1^1/_2$ tablespoons juice. Add the rum, blue curaçao, Hpnotiq and Simple Syrup. Fill the shaker with crushed ice, seal and shake hard for 12 seconds. Pour into the prepared glass and garnish with a slice of star fruit.

Serves 1

PEACH BEURRE BLANC

$1^1/_2$ cups chopped peaches
$^1/_4$ cup chopped shallots
Butter for sautéing
6 tablespoons peach schnapps
$^1/_2$ cup fish stock or clam juice
$^1/_2$ cup apple juice

$^1/_3$ cup honey
2 tablespoons white wine
Cornstarch
Water
$^1/_2$ cup (1 stick) butter,
    chilled and chopped

Sauté the peaches and shallots in a small amount of butter in a saucepan. Add the schnapps, stock, apple juice, honey and wine and stir to loosen the brown bits from the saucepan. Cook until reduced by one-fourth.

Make a slurry of 3 parts cornstarch and 2 parts water in a cup. Add to the peach mixture gradually, cooking until thickened to the desired consistency. Purée the peach mixture in a blender and strain into a bowl, discarding the solids. Whisk in $^1/_2$ cup butter gradually.

Serves 10

Grand Summer Ball

MENU

CIRQUE DE SOLEIL LA SALADE
*Maytag Bleu Cheese Charlotte
presented with a Pear Brandy Poached
Anjou Pear, Chef's Garden Micro Greens
and a Blood Orange Vinaigrette*

BOUEF MAGNIFIQUE
*Grilled Prime Filet of Beef in
a Pinot Noir Sauce*

TRIPOLI LINGUINE
*A seafood medley of scallops, crawfish,
crab and lobster served over squid ink,
beet, saffron and spinach
infused linguine with asparagus*

CHOCOLATE TORTE BRILLANTE

THE GRAND SUMMER BALL

In 1986 a group of community-spirited citizens started the Grand Summer Ball, with the proceeds dedicated to benefit Thomas Hospital. In 1998 the Thomas Hospital Foundation took on the responsibility of the ball and has maintained it ever since. Since 1998, proceeds from the ball have totaled well over $2 million. These proceeds have funded improvements at the hospital, such as an infant and child security system, and have helped to bring open-heart surgery and balloon angioplasty to the people of Baldwin County. The proceeds have also helped fund the new emergency department, renovated a cardiac rehab facility, and helped to purchase digital mammography equipment.

Each year a different Chair and Co-chair help plan the event, which is recognized as one of the most prestigious and successful charitable functions in the area.

Cottages

During summer vacations at the Grand Hotel, lucky families rented out a favorite among guests, the Cottages. The cottages were built after World War II, while renovations were being done to the third hotel. The typical cottage had four bedrooms and two living areas. These could be rented separately, or rented together with a connector door between the two areas. There were eight cottages, three bay-side and five on the lagoon. The cottages were replaced at the turn of the century by the new pool, although they still live on in the memories of the families who enjoyed them.

THE FOURTH OF JULY

Juice drips down the faces of children as they savor the flavor of a freshly sliced watermelon. Barbecues, fireworks, and bonfires are some of the activities that the Grand Hotel loves to host during the Grand Fourth of July celebration. During the day, enjoy the live entertainment out at the Grand pool. Your kids will enjoy the Tom Sawyer Tree House and the slide that they can swish around. Then join the Grand Hotel team in the evening to watch the amazing fireworks while dining on the classic southern barbecue buffet outdoors. Kids' activities are abundant all around the Grand Hotel, so they will never get bored!

APPLE CRANBERRY COBBLER

2 tablespoons butter
6 Granny Smith apples, peeled and
coarsely chopped
12 ounces cranberries
$^3/4$ cup sugar
Juice of 1 lemon
2 teaspoons cinnamon
1$^1/4$ cups cake flour

2 teaspoons baking soda
1 teaspoon salt
$^1/2$ cup (1 stick) butter, softened
$^3/4$ cup sugar
1 egg, beaten
$^1/2$ cup buttermilk
1 teaspoon grated lemon zest

Melt 2 tablespoons butter in a heated skillet. Add the apples, cranberries, $^3/4$ cup sugar, the lemon juice and cinnamon. Sauté for 2 to 4 minutes or until the sugar is caramelized. Spoon into a baking dish.

Mix the cake flour, baking soda and salt together. Cream $^1/2$ cup butter and $^3/4$ cup sugar in a mixing bowl until light and fluffy. Beat in the egg. Add the flour mixture alternately with the buttermilk, adding one-half of each at a time. Stir in the lemon zest.

Spread the batter evenly over the apple mixture. Bake in a preheated 350-degree oven for 30 to 40 minutes or until golden brown. May top with a pie pastry in a lattice pattern instead of the batter topping if desired.

Serves 10

THE GRAND MARGARITA

1 tablespoon Simple Syrup (see page 67)	1/2 ounce Cointreau
Salt for rimming	1/2 ounce Grand Marnier
1/2 lime	2 tablespoon fresh orange juice
1 ounce gold tequila	2 tablespoons Simple Syrup (see page 67)
(tested with José Cuervo Gold)	Crushed ice

Pour 1 tablespoon Simple Syrup onto a shallow plate. Sprinkle salt onto a second shallow plate. Dip the rim of a colored martini glass into the Simple Syrup and then into the salt to rim the glass.

Cut the lime half into three wedges and place in a cocktail shaker. Muddle the lime wedges to release about 1¹/2 tablespoons lime juice. Add the tequila, Cointreau, Grand Marnier, orange juice and 2 tablespoons Simple Syrup. Fill the shaker with crushed ice and shake hard for 12 seconds. Pour into the prepared martini glass.

You may garnish the glass with a lime wedge or orange wedge, if desired.

Serves 1

BLONDIES

2 cups cake flour	6 eggs, beaten
1 cup bread flour	1/2 teaspoon salt
1¹/2 cups (3 sticks) butter, softened	2 tablespoons vanilla extract
3 cups sugar	2 cups chopped pecans

Sift the cake flour and bread flour together. Cream the butter and sugar in a mixing bowl until light and fluffy. Beat in the eggs gradually, mixing well. Stir in the salt and vanilla. Add the flour mixture and mix well. Stir in the pecans.

Spoon into a 9×13-inch baking pan lined on the bottom with baking parchment, spreading the batter evenly into the corners. Bake in a preheated 350-degree oven for 35 minutes or just until set. Cool on a wire rack and cut into squares.

Makes 2 dozen

THE GRAND DINING ROOM

The restaurant title "The Grand Dining Room" has been associated with exquisite cuisine at the Grand Hotel since the mid-1900s. The Grand Dining Room has always lent itself to a feeling of upscale cuisine and Southern grandeur.

In 2008, the Grand Dining Room achieved its highest honor: a four-diamond rating from AAA. Numerous local and state awards have also been given for the unique blend of classic and fusion-style cuisine the menu has boasted. The Grand Dining Room uses the highest-quality, freshest possible ingredients. The Chef's Garden has added crisp herbs, colorful arrays of vegetables, and unique garnishes to our menu. Dinner in the Grand Dining Room begins with a hand-crafted cocktail from the martini cart and a table-side Caesar salad. Dover Sole table-side is a spectacular addition to a grand evening. Be amazed by the sparkle of cinnamon being sprinkled into the flames of the table-side Bananas Foster for the finale. After the evening has concluded, relax in front of the three-sided fireplace in the historic lobby of the hotel or the fire pits outside of Bucky's Birdcage Lounge.

SEAFOOD RISOTTO

Risotto
2 cups arborio rice
1/3 cup chopped onion
1 tablespoon minced garlic
1/4 cup (1/2 stick) butter
1/4 cup white wine
4 cups vegetable stock or
chicken stock
1 cup (4 ounces) finely grated
Parmesan cheese
All-purpose flour for coating
Vegetable oil for deep-frying

Seafood
30 (30- to 40-count) peeled shrimp

20 peeled crawfish tails
10 (20- to 30-count) scallops,
cut into halves
5 ounces crab meat
3 ounces lobster meat, finely chopped
2 tablespoons minced shallots
Vegetable oil for sautéing
1/4 cup brandy
1 1/4 cups Lobster Bisque (page 50)
2 tablespoons basil chiffonade
2 tablespoons lemon juice
Pinch of cayenne pepper
Salt and pepper to taste
Micro greens and large crawfish,
for garnish

For the risotto, sauté the rice with the onion and garlic in the butter in a Dutch oven. Add the wine and stir to loosen the brown bits from the bottom. Add the stock. Bake, covered, in a preheated 350-degree oven for 20 to 30 minutes or until the rice is tender. Remove from the oven and fold in the cheese. Spread the risotto evenly in a rimmed baking sheet sprayed with nonstick cooking spray. Chill until cool and firm. Cut into the desired shapes and coat with flour. Deep-fry the risotto cakes in vegetable oil until crisp on the outside and heated through. Keep warm.

For the seafood, sauté the shrimp, crawfish tails, scallops, crab meat, lobster meat and shallots in a small amount of vegetable oil in a saucepan. Add the brandy and stir to loosen the brown bits from the bottom.

Add the Lobster Bisque, basil, lemon juice and cayenne pepper; mix well. Cook to the thickness of ragoût, stirring constantly. Season with salt and pepper. Place the risotto cakes in serving bowls. Spoon the seafood over the top. Garnish with micro greens and a large crawfish.

Serves 10

ASIAN TUNA

Asian Tuna
1 cup soy sauce
1/3 cup rice wine vinegar
1/3 cup honey
1/4 cup chopped cilantro
1 tablespoon minced garlic
1 tablespoon minced fresh ginger
1/2 teaspoon wasabi
1 teaspoon chili paste
1 1/2 cups sesame oil
1 cup canola oil
10 (6- to 7-ounce) rectangular
pieces ahi tuna

Asian Vegetables
1 cup julienned napa cabbage

1 cup baby corn
1/2 cup bean sprouts
1/2 cup julienned red bell pepper
1/2 cup julienned green bell pepper
1/2 cup julienned yellow bell pepper
1/2 cup julienned red onion
1/2 cup shiitake mushrooms
1/2 cup julienned carrots
1/2 cup snow peas
1/2 cup julienned lotus root
Sesame oil for sautéing

Assembly
Fried cellophane noodles, white and black
    sesame seeds and wasabi oil, for garnish

For the tuna, combine the soy sauce, wine vinegar, honey, cilantro, garlic, ginger, wasabi and chili paste in a bowl. Purée with an immersion blender or hand mixer. Add the sesame oil and canola oil gradually and process with the blender or mixer until emulsified. Pour half the vinaigrette into a container and reserve. Combine the tuna with the remaining vinaigrette in a bowl and marinate in the refrigerator for 2 hours or longer. Remove the tuna from the marinade, discarding the marinade. Sear the tuna in a very hot nonstick ovenproof skillet for 30 seconds on all sides for rare to medium-rare. Place in a preheated 350-degree oven to cook to a greater degree of doneness if desired or in a warm oven to keep warm.

For the vegetables, sauté the cabbage, baby corn, bean sprouts, bell peppers, onion, mushrooms, carrots, snow peas and lotus root in a small amount of sesame oil in a sauté pan. Add a small amount of the reserved vinaigrette and stir to loosen the brown bits from the sauté pan.

To assemble, spoon the remaining reserved vinaigrette onto ten serving plates. Spoon the vegetables into the center of each plate. Arrange the tuna around the vegetables. Garnish with fried cellophane noodles, white and black sesame seeds and wasabi oil.

Serves 10

CRAB CAKES

2 pounds crab meat
1/2 cup finely chopped mixed red, green
and yellow bell peppers
1/3 cup finely chopped red onion
1/4 cup lemon juice
1/4 cup chopped chives
2 tablespoons Cajun seasoning
1 tablespoon Old Bay seasoning

1 tablespoon lemon zest
1 teaspoon cayenne pepper
2 eggs
3/4 cup mayonnaise
2 cups panko
Vegetable oil for sautéing
Julienned carrots, micro greens and
rosemary for garnish

Combine the crab meat, bell peppers, onion, lemon juice, chives, Cajun seasoning, Old Bay seasoning, lemon zest and cayenne pepper in a bowl. Add the eggs and mayonnaise and mix well. Mix in the bread crumbs.

Shape the mixture into twenty cakes. Sauté in a small amount of vegetable oil on an ovenproof griddle or in an ovenproof sauté pan. Place in a preheated 350-degree oven and bake for 3 to 5 minutes or until cooked through. Serve with corn relish and garnish with julienned carrots, micro greens and rosemary.

Serves 10

CREOLE AÏOLI

1/2 cup Creole mustard
1/2 cup mayonnaise
1 tablespoon rice vinegar
1 tablespoon honey

1 teaspoon lemon juice
1 teaspoon chopped garlic
1 teaspoon chopped shallot
Salt and pepper to taste

Combine the Creole mustard, mayonnaise, rice vinegar, honey and lemon juice in a blender. Add the garlic, shallot, salt and pepper. Process until smooth.

Makes about 1/2 cup

PROGRESSIVE WINE LIST AT THE GRAND HOTEL

The Grand Hotel has put in place a Progressive Wine List, which groups the wines by their flavor characteristics from lighter to full body. Wines that share similar tastes are listed near each other. This approach has made wine selection a more enjoyable experience for guests who are interested in trying new and different wines.

As you browse the wine list, you will probably find a wine that you know and enjoy. We recommend at this time that you venture and try another wine or varietal. Utilizing the progressive flavor layout, the selection becomes an effortless, enjoyable experience.

It is simple and fun to read and order from a progressive wine list. Let's say that you are a fan of the cabernet sauvignon grape. As you browse the progressive wine list, you will find three choices for this particular grape:

LIGHT BODY
Cabernet Sauvignon/Shiraz, 2007, Australia

MEDIUM BODY
Cabernet Sauvignon, "Coastal," 2005, California

STRONG BODY
Cabernet Sauvignon, Napa Valley, 2005, California

The placement of these wines we can state the flavor profile of the three. To choose between these wines, you must first understand your flavor profile, which you can do by simply using how you like your coffee as a guide. Let me explain: If you like your coffee with a lot of cream and sugar, you will find the lighter, sweeter-bodied wines more to your liking. If you take your coffee with cream and no sugar, then the full-bodied wines will be a perfect match.

The progressive wine list is designed to make your selection a simple process. It also helps you to venture out and try new varietals. For example, if your taste profile is in the mid-range and you are about to order the Cabernet Sauvignon "Coastal," 2005, California, then take a moment to see what other varietals within your taste profile you can enjoy:

Pinot Noir, Central Coast, 2006, California
Côtes du Rhône, 2004, Rhône, France
Merlot, Reserva, 2005, Central Valley, Chile
Tempranillo, 2006, Rioja, Spain

As you can see, there is more to life than cabernet sauvignon. It is not our intent that you change your liking for any varietal but rather to open up for you a world of opportunity.

THE GRAND HOTEL AWARDS

Zagat's, Top U.S. Hotels, Resorts & Spas

Travel + Leisure's Top 50 Family Resorts

Winner of AAA's Four-Diamond Award

Winner of AAA's Four-Diamond Award for the Grand Dining Room

Reader's Choice, Meeting South Magazine
Food & Beverage Excellence Award

Top 3% Both Event & Guest Satisfaction,
Marriott Hotels, Resorts & Suites

Best of the South Award, *Meetings Media*

Golf Tee Award for Excellence in Golf & Meeting Facilities,
Meetings & Conventions Magazine

#2 in the Top 21 Romantic Places for "I Do," *Brides Magazine*

#1 "Five Great Summer Vacations That Don't Cost a Bundle,"
Fox News

Marriott Full Service General Manager Awards, Central Region –
"Spirit to Serve Our Communities"

Winner of the Readers' Choice Award
presented by *Mobile Press-Register*

Winner of the Readers' Choice Award presented by *Southern Living*

Director of Sales of the Year, Franchise Hotels,
Central Region, Marriott Hotels, Resorts & Suites

Director of Sales of the Year for North American Lodging Operations,
Marriott Hotels, Resorts & Suites

Best Spas USA: *The Guidebook to Luxury Resort,
Hotel & Destination Spas*

Taste of Mobile Awards, "Best Seafood" & "Best Pasta Dish" –
Saltwater Grill

Taste of Mobile Awards, "Top Dessert" – Grand Dining Room

Mobile Chef's Challenge Award for Best Seafood & Best Appetizer

Alabama Restaurant Manager of the Year Finalist
(Stars of Hospitality)

Alabama Hotelier of the Year Finalist (Stars of Hospitality)

Alabama Chef of the Year Finalist (Stars of Hospitality)

#2 Property Rank within Marriott Resort Brand

#1 Ranked Breakfast within Marriott Hotels, Resorts & Suites

#5 Ranked Overall Quality of Food within
Marriott Hotels, Resorts & Suites

Top Property Rank based on Guest Survey Satisfaction
within Marriott Hotels, Resorts & Suites

Award of Unique Distinction presented by
Wine Enthusiast's Magazine

"Reader's Choice Award Winner" by the *ConventionSouth*
readers for all 8 of the PCH Hotels and Resorts,
including the Grand Hotel Marriott Resort

Pinnacle Award presented by *Successful Meetings Magazine*

Golf Magazines Silver Medal Award

100 Best Golf Shops in America

THE LOUIS FLEISCHER MEMORIAL FISHING PIER

On June 14, 1994, the Grand Hotel's fishing pier was dedicated to the memory of Louis Fleischer.

For over twenty-five years Mr. and Mrs. Fleischer came to the Grand Hotel several times each year to enjoy the resort and relax from the hard work of their dry goods store in Shaw, Mississippi. During each stay with us, Louis would spend every morning and afternoon fishing from the pier. His wife, Fan Joe, would join him each day for lunch on the pier and then they would dine in the Grand Dining Room each evening, enjoying the fish that Louis had caught during the day.

After a short illness in 1986, Louis passed away in Greenville, Mississippi, where they had moved several months before to retire. Fan Joe continued to visit the hotel several times a year and was truly one of our most beloved guests. This dedication is a tribute to a wonderful man and a loving husband . . . he will always be missed by the staff of our resort.

to the grand Hotel, if you see a school of fish call me and I will bring my castnet and catch them in my castnet and bring it to someone then they will bring it to the grand Hotel and cook it for someone that if they order some thing that Goes with fish make it for them if you see another school of fish call me.

Letter written by Benjamin Herzog
Age 6

Point Clear Frittata

2 tablespoons finely chopped tomato
2 tablespoons finely chopped canned
   artichoke hearts
$1/2$ cup spinach leaves, chopped
$1 1/2$ ounces crab meat
1 tablespoon chopped scallions

Butter for sautéing
Salt and pepper
3 eggs, beaten
2 tablespoons shredded Parmesan cheese
Chopped tomato and watercress,
   for garnish

Sauté 2 tablespoons chopped tomato, the artichoke hearts, spinach, crab meat and scallions in a small amount of butter in an ovenproof omelet pan until the vegetables are tender. Season with salt and pepper. Add the eggs and cook until soft-set, stirring frequently. Stir in the cheese.

Place the pan in a 350-degree oven to melt the cheese and set the eggs to the desired degree of doneness. Garnish with additional tomato and watercress.

You can also spoon the soft-set eggs into a mold and unmold in a serving ramekin to finish.

Serves 1

FRESHLY BAKED SCONES

4 cups all-purpose flour	1/2 cup raisins, dried cherries, dried cranberries or currants
6 tablespoons sugar	1 egg
2 1/2 tablespoons baking powder	1 1/4 cups half-and-half
1 teaspoon grated orange zest	2 teaspoons vanilla extract
Pinch of salt	1 egg
6 tablespoons butter, chilled and cut into cubes	Milk
	Sugar for sprinkling

Mix the flour, 6 tablespoons sugar, the baking powder, orange zest and salt in a bowl. Add the butter and cut in with a pastry blender or two knives until pea-size crumbs form. Stir in the raisins.

Combine the egg, half-and-half and vanilla in a bowl and mix well. Add three-fourths of the flour mixture and mix well. Add the remaining flour mixture gradually, mixing to form a smooth dough.

Roll on a lightly floured surface and cut into circles. Arrange on a baking sheet lined with baking parchment. Beat the egg with enough milk to measure 1/4 cup. Brush over the scones. Sprinkle with additional sugar. Bake in a preheated 375-degree oven for 10 to 12 minutes or until light golden brown.

Serves 10

The smell of freshly brewed coffee and delicious cookies at 4:00 p.m. brings children and adults to the historic main building for one of the Grand Hotel's favorite traditions . . . afternoon tea. In 1968 the restaurant manager, Alfred Agee, created teatime so that hotel guests would gather in a central location after they checked in so that he could make their reservations for the dining room. Before 1980, most guests would stay for weeks at a time, so it was important to actually reserve one table for them for the rest of their stay. The afternoon tea tradition continues today but has grown into much more. We not only have coffee but have expanded to include hot chocolate, scones, cookies, clotted cream, and steaming orange pekoe tea. Bucky's Birdcage Lounge has long been the gathering place for friends and families, who sip on tea while the kids enjoy the putting green lawn.

SEAFOOD BOIL

3 gallons water
2 cups white wine
1 bunch celery, coarsely
  chopped
1/2 bunch parsley
2 onions, cut into quarters
3 sprigs of thyme
1 tablespoon peppercorns
2/3 cup crab boil or
  Cajun seasoning
2 1/2 pounds whole red
  bliss potatoes
10 ears of corn, cut
  into halves

50 (16- to 20-count)
  unpeeled shrimp
1 1/2 pounds sausage, cut
  diagonally into 1 1/2-inch
  pieces (tested with
  Conecuh)
3/4 cup (1 1/2 sticks) butter,
  chopped
1/4 cup Cajun seasoning
10 tablespoons hot sauce
Salt and pepper to taste
Boiled crab claws and lemon
  wedges, for garnish

Combine the water, wine, celery, parsley, onions, thyme and peppercorns in a stockpot. Bring to a boil. Reduce the heat and simmer for 30 minutes. Strain the mixture and return the liquid to the stockpot; discard the solids. Stir in the crab boil.

Bring to a boil and add the potatoes and corn. Cook for 20 minutes or until the potatoes are nearly tender. Add the shrimp and sausage and cook for 5 to 8 minutes or until the shrimp and sausage are cooked through and the potatoes are tender.

Strain the mixture and return the vegetables and seafood to the stockpot; discard the cooking liquid. Stir in the butter, Cajun seasoning, hot sauce, salt and pepper. Cook until heated through and coated evenly. Garnish with boiled crab claws and lemon wedges. Serve with crusty bread and lemonade.

Serves 10

MONARCH BUTTERFLIES

On the long list of repeat visitors, the monarch butterflies may hold the record for number of visits. Each year in October and November, the beautiful monarchs stop by on their 3,000-mile journey from Canada to the Yucatan Peninsula's Sierra Madre mountains. They rest and feed on the nectar from the lemon bottlebrush bushes, pentas, and lantana. Point Clear is the last landmass where they gather before crossing the Gulf of Mexico. Many Grand Hotel guests choose the monarch time to visit with cameras and binoculars in hand. It's true that "butterflies are free" at the Grand—free for observation and for continuing on their journey.

The Ringing of the Sunset Bell
A Southern tradition that signals
the end of the day and beginning of
the night . . . Let the bell's toll move
you to the porch of Bucky's Birdcage
Lounge to enjoy a spectacular
Mobile Bay sunset. The sunset is so
beautiful; we had to concoct a drink
in honor of it . . . the Mobile Bay
Sunset, touting the same gorgeous
colors displayed in the sky. We begin
our celebration and daily ringing of
the bell thirty minutes before sunset,
so get there early!

MOBILE BAY SUNSET

1 ounce vodka
$1/4$ cup fresh lime juice
$1/4$ cup fresh orange juice
$1/4$ cup pineapple juice
Crushed ice
1 ounce grenadine
Orange wedge, for garnish

Combine the vodka, lime juice, orange juice and
pineapple juice in a cocktail shaker. Fill the
shaker with crushed ice; seal and shake hard
for 12 seconds. Pour into a highball glass
and top with the grenadine. Garnish with an
orange wedge.

Serves 1

THANKSGIVING

Thanksgiving marks the beginning of a very active holiday season at the Grand Hotel. Working day and night, our chefs prepare food for more than 1,200 people for our Thanksgiving Day Brunch, which is offered in both our Grand Ballroom and Grand Dining Room. After the delicious buffet, guests participate in our many activities. Upon request, the Grand Hotel turkey will visit each child's room and tuck him or her in. The next morning the guests are amazed by the hotel's transformation into a Christmas Wonderland. Families gather at the twenty-five-foot Christmas tree that has magically appeared overnight. The dining room is completely decorated with red bows and large live wreaths placed throughout. The award-winning breakfast buffet now has a large-size gingerbread village complete with the "North Pool" and a statue of Bucky Miller. The day after Thanksgiving is the traditional "Lighting of the Trees," where the live oaks are adorned with millions of Christmas lights.

GREEN BEAN CASSEROLE

Fried Onion Rings
1 yellow onion
1/2 cup all-purpose flour
1/4 teaspoon Cajun seasoning
1/4 teaspoon salt
1/8 teaspoon pepper
Vegetable oil for frying

Green Bean Casserole
1 cup chopped bacon
1 cup chopped onion
2 pounds fresh or frozen whole green
    beans, trimmed
2 cups chicken stock or turkey stock
Cornstarch
Water
1 cup half-and-half or heavy cream

For the onion rings, slice the onion into very thin rings. Mix the flour, Cajun seasoning, salt and pepper in a bowl. Add the onion rings and toss to coat well; shake off any excess flour mixture. Fry in a skillet in vegetable oil preheated to 350 degrees until golden brown. Drain.

For the casserole, sauté the bacon in a small stockpot until crisp and light brown. Add the chopped onion and sauté for 2 to 3 minutes or until caramelized. Add the green beans and sauté for 2 to 3 minutes. Add the stock and bring to a boil.

Make a 2- to 3-ounce slurry of three parts cornstarch and two parts water in a cup. Add to the bean mixture and cook until thickened, stirring constantly. Add the half-and-half and bring to a boil.

Spoon into a buttered baking dish. Bake, covered, in a preheated 350-degree oven for 30 minutes. Top with the Fried Onion Rings and bake, uncovered, for 10 minutes longer.

Serves 10

HERB BREAD STUFFING

5 cups coarsely chopped French bread
1/3 cup butter, melted
1 cup finely chopped onion
1 cup chopped celery
1 tablespoon minced garlic
Olive oil for sautéing
3 cups crumbled corn bread

1/3 cup chopped fresh parsley
1 tablespoon chopped fresh sage
1 tablespoon chopped fresh thyme
1 tablespoon poultry seasoning
Salt and pepper to taste
3 cups turkey stock or chicken stock

Toss the French bread with the butter in a bowl, coating evenly. Spread on a baking sheet and bake in a preheated 350-degree oven until light brown. Maintain the oven temperature.

Sauté the onion, celery and garlic in a small amount of olive oil in a saucepan over medium heat for 1 to 2 minutes. Add the toasted French bread, corn bread, parsley, sage, thyme, poultry seasoning, salt and pepper; mix well. Sauté for 2 to 3 minutes. Add the stock and cook for 3 to 4 minutes.

Spoon the stuffing into a buttered baking dish and bake for 25 to 30 minutes or until golden brown.

Serves 10

POTATOES AU GRATIN

6 Idaho potatoes, peeled and
thinly sliced
1 cup heavy cream
1 cup half-and-half
3 eggs, beaten
3/4 cup (1 1/2 sticks) butter, melted

1 cup (4 ounces) grated Parmesan cheese
1 1/2 tablespoons minced garlic
1 1/2 teaspoons minced rosemary
1 1/2 teaspoons minced thyme
Salt and pepper to taste
3/4 cup (3 ounces) grated Parmesan cheese

Combine the potatoes with the cream, half-and-half, eggs, butter, 1 cup cheese, the garlic, rosemary, thyme, salt and pepper in a bowl; mix to coat the potatoes evenly.

Spoon the potato mixture evenly into a buttered baking dish. Bake, covered, in a preheated 350-degree oven for 45 to 50 minutes or until the potatoes are tender. Sprinkle with 3/4 cup cheese. Broil until golden brown. Cool slightly before serving.

Serves 10

ACORN SQUASH TASTER WITH
CINNAMON AND NUTMEG WHIPPED CREAM

2 acorn squash	1 teaspoon cinnamon
1/3 cup packed brown sugar	1 teaspoon nutmeg
1/4 cup chopped shallots	1/2 teaspoon white pepper
3 tablespoons butter	Whipped cream
3 tablespoons brandy	Cinnamon for sprinkling
2 cups chicken stock	Nutmeg for sprinkling
2 cups heavy cream	

Cut the squash into halves, discarding the seeds. Sprinkle the brown sugar into the squash cavities and place on a baking sheet. Roast in a preheated 375-degree oven for 25 to 30 minutes or until tender.

Sauté the shallots in the butter in a stockpot until translucent. Scoop out the cooked squash into the stockpot and cook for 2 minutes. Add the brandy, stirring to loosen the brown bits from the stockpot. Stir in the stock, heavy cream, 1 teaspoon cinnamon, 1 teaspoon nutmeg and the white pepper. Cook over low heat for 3 to 4 minutes longer.

Purée the squash mixture in a blender or food processor and strain through a china cap. Return to the stockpot and heat to serving temperature.

Serve warm in shot glasses. Top with whipped cream and sprinkle with additional cinnamon and nutmeg.

Serves 10

The Grand Band
Sage A. "Jack" Normand was a popular pianist with a band in
New Orleans when Ed Roberts, owner of the Grand Hotel, asked him to play for the
re-opening of the hotel in April of 1941. Jack's band played off and on until after
World War II. In 1951, Mr. Roberts convinced Jack to move to the area and become the
resident orchestra leader. The Grand Hotel orchestra was a big attraction as an
entertaining and friendly family band. Guests were always amazed that Jack would
remember their favorite songs and play them as he saw them enter the room.

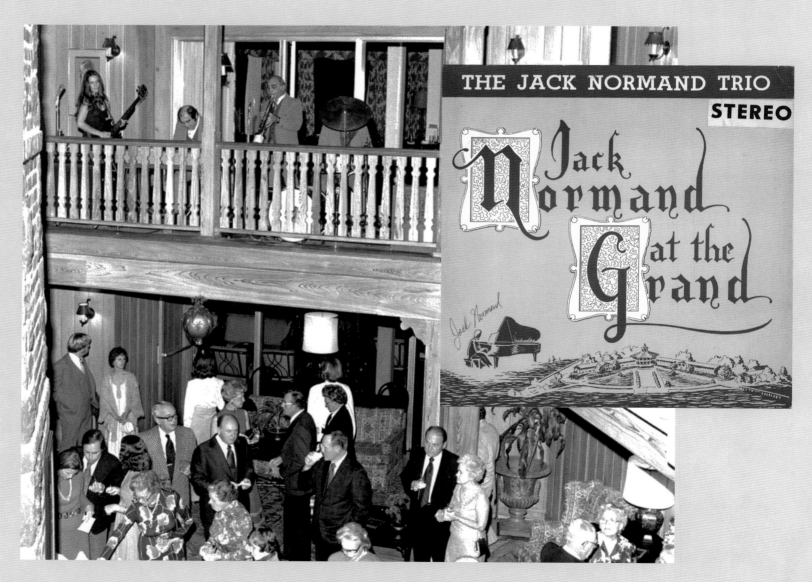

THE GRAND HOTEL

Culinary Academy

Each month a Grand chef at the Grand Hotel Marriott Resort, Golf Club, & Spa will be teaching classes at the resort's Culinary Academy. The classes are aimed at expanding the participants' knowledge of the culinary basics and then incorporating more advanced techniques. Whether you are a beginner or an expert in the kitchen, the chef's classes are fun, hands-on experiences that will have people raving about your culinary skills.

In each Grand Culinary Academy, you will receive a two-hour cooking demonstration, recipes, food sampling, and a diploma.

Classes are on the third Saturday of the month at 10:00 a.m. and are limited in size.

Cooking Essentials I: Intro to Cooking

Even if you have been cooking for years, a Grand chef will offer many insights and secrets that you can use at home. Here is a sampling of what you will learn: how to hold a knife, knife cuts, how to sharpen a knife, culinary do's and don'ts, sanitation, and nutrition.

Cooking Essentials II: Soups

Soups should be an essential part of your diet. They will keep you warm in the winter months and complement salads in the summer. The menu for this Academy includes Loaded Baked Potato, Gazpacho, and Grand Gumbo. Dazzle your friends and family when you use your new "gourmet cooking skills" at home.

Cooking Essentials III: Salads

Salads are a must for any time of the year and bring balance to your diet. In this class learn how to prepare Baby Mixed Greens with Goat Cheese and a Strawberry-Poppy Seed Vinaigrette, Spinach Salad with a Hot Bacon-Dijon Dressing, and Grand Marnier-Macerated Tropical Fruit Salad with Wild Berry Yogurt Sauce.

Cooking Essentials IV: Entrées ~ Sauté

Learn the art of sautéing, meaning "to jump," while being taught the step-by-step process of making the following dishes . . . Sautéed Chicken Breast with a Sun-dried Tomato Cream Sauce, Teriyaki Glazed Flank Steak and Plantation Shrimp Pasta.

Cooking Essentials V: Grilling Basics

Prepare yourself for the summer grilling season. A Grand chef will

Family Fun Cooking

Take a break from the Grand's signature pools and learn to prepare a variety of foods with your children. Young children and the young-at-heart will help prepare a variety of great summer dishes. Children attend this class for free.

How to Make a Gourmet Lunch

A Grand chef teaches you how to prepare gourmet lunches at home. The menu includes an exotic Oriental Chicken Salad with a lavish Fresh Tropical Fruit Cocktail and a Grand Marnier Zabaglione for dessert.

Cooking Essentials VI: Baking Basics

Enjoy learning how to make a variety of breads, including sourdough, French, and our own Grand loaf. Learn the basics of bread dough preparation. After you are finished, you will have a fresh loaf of bread to take home and share.

Wine Class with Gourmet Cheeses

This class is perfect for the wine lover, whether a novice or an expert. We will be tasting and discussing wine varieties. Learn insights on how to choose the perfect wine, and then how to pair it with food. The growing regions of wine will be discussed while you sample gourmet cheeses from around the world.

Cooking Essentials VII: Pastry Basics

A Grand chef will share the secrets of preparing the top three classic French pastry recipes of all time. The menu includes Crème Brûlée, Mousses, and Bananas Foster. These rich gourmet desserts will be an instant success when served to your guests.

How to Cook a Thanksgiving Dinner

One step at a time, a Grand chef will teach you how to prepare a remarkable Thanksgiving meal for your VIP guests. A grocery list will be provided to ensure you have all the needed ingredients on hand. He will then take you through each course—salad, entrée, starch, vegetable, and dessert. Leave confident in preparing this wonderful meal, while saving both time and money. This year you can actually enjoy preparing your Thanksgiving meal.

How to Make a Gingerbread House

Learn step-by-step instructions on how to build and decorate your own gingerbread house. Get in the holiday spirit and leave with a gingerbread house creation of your own. Children receive a half-price discount on this fun and festive class.

THE GRAND HOTEL
Culinary Academy

Each month a Grand chef at the Grand Hotel Marriott Resort, Golf Club, & Spa will be teaching classes at the resort's Culinary Academy. The classes are aimed at expanding the participants' knowledge of the culinary basics and then incorporating more advanced techniques. Whether you are a beginner or expert in the kitchen, the chef's classes are fun, hands-on experiences that will have people raving about your culinary skills.

In each Grand Culinary Academy, you will receive a two-hour cooking demonstration, recipes, food sampling, and a diploma. Classes are on the third Saturday of the month at 10:00 a.m. and are limited in size.

CHRISTMAS

Gathering the family for the holidays is a tradition the Grand Hotel is famous for. Starting the day after Thanksgiving, the Grand Hotel transforms with Christmas décor. The twenty-five-foot Christmas tree is just a couple of inches shy of touching the ceiling in the historic main lobby and lights placed on the magnificent oaks sparkle throughout the hotel grounds.

Breakfast with Santa has been a fun family tradition that many have raved about as "magical." Children gather around the main lobby to sit in Santa's lap and whisper their Christmas present wishes. The smell of waffles and omelets fills the room as families enjoy the award-winning breakfast buffet, which is displayed around the large-scale gingerbread village of the Grand Hotel (equipped with the "North Pool" and statue of Bucky Miller!).

Family activities during Christmas include the silver bell guessing, coloring contest, gingerbread house building, feeding the ducks, riding bikes, decorating Christmas stockings and ornaments, playing croquet, and one of the kids' favorites, the "elf tuck-in" on Christmas Eve . . . just to name a few!

"The twenty-five-foot Christmas tree is just a couple of inches shy of touching the ceiling in the historic main lobby . . ."

APPLE PIE EGGNOG À LA MODE

1¹/2 cups finely
chopped peeled
apples
1 tablespoon butter
¹/3 cup sugar
1 teaspoon cinnamon
¹/4 teaspoon nutmeg
Pinch of ground
allspice

¹/2 cup apple brandy
(tested with
Calvados)
2 cups milk
2 cups half-and-half
6 eggs, beaten
1 teaspoon vanilla
extract
Whipped cream

Sauté the apples in the butter in a saucepan over medium heat
for 2 to 3 minutes. Stir in the sugar, cinnamon, nutmeg and
allspice. Add the brandy and stir to loosen the brown bits from
the saucepan.

Add the milk and half-and-half to the apples and bring to a
simmer. Whisk about half the hot milk mixture gradually into
the beaten eggs. Whisk constantly, being careful not to
scramble the eggs. Stir the tempered egg mixture back into
the remaining apple mixture. Cook until thickened, whisking
constantly. Stir in the vanilla. Remove from the heat.

Spoon the eggnog into individual containers and chill in the
refrigerator for 8 hours or longer. Serve warm or chilled,
topped with whipped cream.

Serves 10

The Grand Hotel lobby

GINGERBREAD COOKIES

6 cups all-purpose flour
1 tablespoon baking powder
1 teaspoon nutmeg
$1^1/2$ teaspoons cinnamon
1 tablespoon ginger
$1/2$ teaspoon salt
1 cup shortening

1 cup packed brown sugar
1 cup molasses
$1/2$ cup water
1 egg
2 teaspoons vanilla extract
Royal Icing (below)

Mix the flour, baking powder, nutmeg, cinnamon, ginger and salt together. Melt the shortening in a large saucepan. Combine with the brown sugar, molasses, water, egg and vanilla in the bowl of a standing mixer and mix well. Add the dry ingredients and mix well. Roll $1/4$ inch thick on a floured surface. Cut into the desired shapes. Place on a cookie sheet and bake in a preheated 350- to 375-degree oven for 10 to 12 minutes or until brown. Decorate with Royal Icing.

Makes 6 dozen

ROYAL ICING

$2^1/2$ cups (or more) confectioners' sugar
2 (or more) egg whites

$1/4$ teaspoon cream of tartar
$1/2$ teaspoon vanilla extract

Combine the confectioners' sugar, egg whites, cream of tartar and vanilla in a mixing bowl. Beat at low speed for 5 minutes. Increase the speed to high and beat until stiff peaks form. Add additional confectioners' sugar for a thicker icing or egg whites for a thinner icing.

If you are concerned about using uncooked egg whites, use whites from eggs pasteurized in their shells, which are sold at some speciality food stores, or use an equivalent amount of meringue powder and follow the package directions.

Makes about $2^1/2$ cups

Gingerbread Village at the Grand

THE GRAND EXPANSION...

At the heart of the Colony at the Grand are the Lakewood Club amenities.

The amenities center opened in 2009 and is a reflection of style and substance, featuring a clubhouse with vaulted timber-beamed ceilings, a lodge-style wood-burning fireplace, and overstuffed leather chairs. A bit nearer to the edge of the lake sits the incredible custom-designed aquatics complex positioned around a signature fountain. The aquatics complex also boasts waterfalls, a hot tub, a lap pool, a slow-current lazy river, and a luxurious shallow-water wading shelf perfect for sunning and dipping a hand into the crystal water. For the kids, there is an eighty-foot water-slide, a "spray-ground," and water cannons that are sure to please. The complex is flanked on one side by a fully featured table-service restaurant and on the other by well-equipped fitness facilities. Facilities include steam rooms, separate men's and women's locker rooms, a motion studio, cardio machines, and personalized instruction. As a final touch, a giant window wall provides panoramic views across the pools, the beach, and the lake, making this the perfect place to hone both body and mind.